UDK iOS Game Development Beginner's Guide

Create your own third-person shooter game using the Unreal Development Kit to create your own game on Apple's iOS devices, such as the iPhone, iPad and iPod Touch

John P. Doran

Christos Gatzidis

BIRMINGHAM - MUMBAI

UDK iOS Game Development Beginner's Guide

First published: August 2012

Production Reference: 1190812

Published by Packt Publishing Ltd.
Livery Place
35 Livery Street
Birmingham B3 2PB, UK.

ISBN 978-1-84969-190-1

www.packtpub.com

Cover Image by John Preston Doran (netravelr@gmail.com)

Credits

Authors

John P. Doran

Christos Gatzidis

Reviewers

Richard Moore

Dan Weiss

Acquisition Editor

Joanna Finchen

Lead Technical Editor

Unnati Shah

Technical Editors

Prasanna Joglekar

Prashant Salvi

Project Coordinator

Vishal Bodwani

Proofreader

Maria Gould

Indexer

Rekha Nair

Production Coordinator

Melwyn D'sa

Cover Work

Melwyn D'sa

About the Authors

John Doran is a 23 year old Technical Game Designer, who has worked on all manners of educational, mod, and professional game projects. He graduated from DigiPen Institute of Technology in Redmond, WA with a Bachelor of Science in Game Design. John previously worked at LucasArts in San Francisco, CA on *Star Wars 1313* as an Intern-Level Designer. He is currently working at DigiPen's campus in Singapore tutoring and assisting students while giving lectures on UDK, Flash, and Actionscript. If you would like to reach him, send him an e-mail at john@johnpdoran.com. Though John occasionally writes papers which he posts on his personal website, this is his first published book.

I would first like to thank both Christos Gatzidis and Joanna Finchen, for giving me the opportunity to write this book. I would also like to thank all of the people at Packt, including Vishal Bodwani and Unnati Shah, for all their support during the writing process, you were all so amazing!

I would also like to thank Daniel Weiss. In addition to being a Technical Reviewer of the book, he helped me when I was just learning Unreal Tournament 3 and kindled my love of Epic's fine game engine without which I wouldn't be here today.

On that same note, I also want to thank Samir Abou Samra and Elie Hosry for their support and encouragement while working on this book, and the rest of the DigiPenSingapore staff including Jocelyn Villanueva, Chris Champagne, and Nicolette Oh, as well as my Singapore friends, Josë Rivero, Matt Hill, and Gabriel Serra.

Last but not least, a big thanks goes to all of my friends, my little brothers and sister, Chris, Joey, and Dymphna Doran, and my girlfriend Hannah Mai for being patient with me, as I spent my free time and weekends away from them as I finished the last few chapters of the book. Finally, my parents, Joseph and Sandra Doran took me seriously, when I told them I wanted to make games.

Dr. Christos Gatzidis is a Senior Lecturer in Creative Technology at Bournemouth University, UK at the School of Design, Engineering, and Computing. He has a Ph.D. from City University London, UK and an M.Sc. in Computer Animation from Teesside University, UK, and has previously published work in a number of academic edited books, conferences, and journals. He is also the framework leader for the Creative Technology collection of degrees at Bournemouth University (which includes the B.Sc. in Games Technology and the M.Sc. in Computer Games Technology courses). Christos teaches a variety of units on these courses and uses Epic's UDK across all years of the undergraduate course, to cover topics ranging from basic level design fundamentals to more advanced scripting.

I would like to thank all friends, colleagues, and family who offered support during the writing of this book and, of course, the great people at Packt (for their guidance and endless patience) plus, last but not least, Epic Games (for the creation of UDK, easily one of the coolest game design tools ever)!

About the Reviewers

Richard Moore graduated in 2009 studying video games design at Hull School of Art and Design, where he first began expanding his creativity by working as a web designer in Hull, East Yorkshire, and London for 3 years. He worked on a number of different projects with clients from different industry backgrounds, such as a collection of stylish websites, logos, brochures, business cards, web banners, animated graphics, and e-mail marketing campaigns. Through the clouds lies his passion in video game development and the complete creation of 3D art including modeling, texturing, and high resolution rendering. He does game documentation and conceptual drawings as well.

Richard will always take any opportunity to meet as many different people from the game development community as possible and as a result, he has attended the Game Grads career fair, participated in the Game Republic 2009 student showcase in Sheffield and Platform 2010, Hulls 1st Digital and Gaming event where he won the award for best character and a cheque for £100. In March 2011, he was involved in Platform Expo's 2011, Hull's second video game expo, where he entered the video game showcase for the second consecutive year and won second prize for his outstanding contribution to video game design, and is now involved in Platform Expo's 2012 being held at the University of Hull.

In July 2011, he volunteered as a Marketing Assistant/Designer for an online-based video games magazine, where he would assist the Editor-In-Chief in designing templates for latest issues of the magazine, writing reviews on latest video game titles, and talking to clients about potential advertising coverage within the magazine and online. As a result, he is now working as a Games Designer/Developer for Concise Media Design based in London, who create ground-breaking iPad apps, high-impact short films, and bespoke video games. In his spare time, he focuses on more freelance design and development work with up and coming companies, as well as rambling on about video games.

Dan Weiss is currently a programmer working at Psyonix Studios in San Diego, CA. He is a 2010 graduate of DigiPen Institute of Technology, having worked on titles such as *Attack of the 50ft Robot!* during his time there. Since 2004, he has also been working on the Unreal Engine, producing the mod *Unreal Demolition* for Unreal Tournament 2004 and Unreal Tournament 3, and is currently working on the iOS title *ARC Squadron*.

I'd like to thank my parents for believing in my crazy idea of working on videogames for a living; Rachel Rutherford for always being available at all hours of the day when I need some advice; and John Doran for thinking of me when this book started coming together, and always providing me with some laughs about his latest Kismet tricks.

www.PacktPub.com

Support files, eBooks, discount offers and more

You might want to visit www.PacktPub.com for support files and downloads related to your book.

Did you know that Packt offers eBook versions of every book published, with PDF and ePub files available? You can upgrade to the eBook version at www.PacktPub.com and as a print book customer, you are entitled to a discount on the eBook copy. Get in touch with us at service@packtpub.com for more details.

At www.PacktPub.com, you can also read a collection of free technical articles, sign up for a range of free newsletters and receive exclusive discounts and offers on Packt books and eBooks.

http://PacktLib.PacktPub.com

Do you need instant solutions to your IT questions? PacktLib is Packt's online digital book library. Here, you can access, read and search across Packt's entire library of books.

Why Subscribe?

- Fully searchable across every book published by Packt
- Copy and paste, print and bookmark content
- On demand and accessible via web browser

Free Access for Packt account holders

If you have an account with Packt at www.PacktPub.com, you can use this to access PacktLib today and view nine entirely free books. Simply use your login credentials for immediate access.

Table of Contents

Preface

It has never been a more attractive time to be an app developer. With no signs of stopping, Apple's iOS devices are dominating the mobile scene and with UDK, the free version of the most popular third-party game engine available, it has never been easier to get into the app business.

This book, *UDK iOS Game Development Beginner's Guide*, takes a clear, step-by-step approach to building a small third-person shooter game using the Unreal Development Kit with plenty of examples of how to create a game that is uniquely your own.

You will begin learning the fundamentals of the Unreal Engine before creating a third-person shooter game in UDK. After the game is created you will learn what can be done with any project to optimize your game for the iOS platform and discover special considerations that need to be made. Finally, you'll publish your game on the App Store for the world to see and play along, with details on the different costs associated with publishing.

What this book covers

Chapter 1, *Getting Started on UDK with iOS*, offers a brief overview of the exciting world that is UDK development for iOS, while also using UDK Remote to play UDK games on PC using our iOS device as the input device.

Chapter 2, *Beginning Urban Warrior: A Third Person Shooter*, gives readers an insight into UDK's interface, starting off building a room, adding lighting, and populating the room with models.

Chapter 3, *Taking It to the Next level: Enriching with Content*, adds an exterior to our level while also adding lighting and fog specifically for mobile devices. Readers also use the Mobile Preview option to show how our level looks on an iOS device, while breathing life into our world with particle systems.

Chapter 4, Using Kismet and Matinee, allows us to look at Kismet and Matinee, two of the most popular ways to create motion and interactivity in our otherwise static world, creating a cinematic, an automatic door, and adding functionality to our game using Mobile Input. We also learn about sequence objects made specifically for mobile devices.

Chapter 5, Action Sequences for Urban Warrior, teaches readers about sequences, subsequences, and prefabs, while developing combat scenarios for our game with AI enemies.

Chapter 6, Bringing it all together, shows how to rapidly prototype levels using a workflow using Geometry Mode to flesh out Urban Warrior into a completed level.

Chapter 7, Advanced Content Creation for Urban Warrior, discusses how to make the game your own by bringing in custom content to your game, such as a main menu, audio, textures, static meshes, as well as how to create materials that work the same way on both PC and iOS, with some tips for optimization and debugging for iOS games.

Chapter 8, Publishing and Monetizing your Game, takes your finished game and walks through the process of getting the game onto your own device, and eventually to the iOS App Store, discussing all you need to know about the royalties model Epic Games has in place for UDK-developed iOS titles, with links leading readers who are interested to learn about adding even more functionality to their game.

What you need for this book

In order to use this book you need to have a computer with Windows that is capable of running the Unreal Development Kit (UDK). UDK requires a personal computer with the following system configuration:

- Windows XP SP3 (32-bit only) with DirectX 9.0c
- 2GHz or better CPU
- 2+ GB RAM
- A graphics card with Shader Model 3.0 support, such as nVidia GeForce 7800

Note that Windows 7 64-bit is currently the mainstream development environment.

The following are the requirements for content development:

- Windows 7 64-bit
- 2.0+ GHz multi-core processor
- 8 GB System RAM
- NVIDIA 8000 series or higher graphics card
- Plenty of HDD space

The UDK will install .NET Framework 3.5 Service Pack 1, if you don't already have it, which will require an internet connection.

Who this book is for

If you would like to make iOS games with the Unreal Development Kit, or are interested in porting your game from PC to iOS, this book is for you. This book assumes no prior knowledge of UDK, so is a good starting off point for learning UDK as well, though with more emphasis towards building games specifically for the iOS platform.

Conventions

In this book, you will find several headings appearing frequently.

To give clear instructions of how to complete a procedure or task, we use:

Time for action – heading

1. Action 1

2. Action 2

3. Action 3

Instructions often need some extra explanation so that they make sense, so they are followed with:

What just happened?

This heading explains the working of tasks or instructions that you have just completed.

You will also find some other learning aids in the book, including:

Pop quiz – heading

These are short multiple choice questions intended to help you test your own understanding.

Have a go hero – heading

These set practical challenges and give you ideas for experimenting with what you have learned.

You will also find a number of styles of text that distinguish between different kinds of information. Here are some examples of these styles, and an explanation of their meaning.

New terms and **important words** are shown in bold. Words that you see on the screen, in menus or dialog boxes for example, appear in the text like this: " From the top menu, select **View | Viewport Configuration | 2x1 Split**."

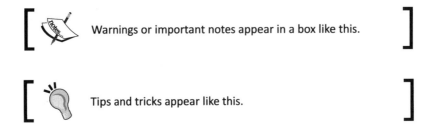

> Warnings or important notes appear in a box like this.

> Tips and tricks appear like this.

Reader feedback

Feedback from our readers is always welcome. Let us know what you think about this book—what you liked or may have disliked. Reader feedback is important for us to develop titles that you really get the most out of.

To send us general feedback, simply send an e-mail to feedback@packtpub.com, and mention the book title through the subject of your message.

If there is a topic that you have expertise in and you are interested in either writing or contributing to a book, see our author guide on www.packtpub.com/authors.

Customer support

Now that you are the proud owner of a Packt book, we have a number of things to help you to get the most from your purchase.

Downloading the example code

You can download the example code files for all Packt books you have purchased from your account at http://www.packtpub.com. If you purchased this book elsewhere, you can visit http://www.packtpub.com/support and register to have the files e-mailed directly to you.

Downloading the color images of this book

We also provide you a PDF fi le that has color images of the screenshots used in this book. The color images will help you bet er understand the changes in the output. You can download this file from http://downloads.packtpub.com/sites/default/files/downloads/1901EXP_UDK iPhone Game,Development.pdf

Errata

Although we have taken every care to ensure the accuracy of our content, mistakes do happen. If you find a mistake in one of our books—maybe a mistake in the text or the code—we would be grateful if you would report this to us. By doing so, you can save other readers from frustration and help us improve subsequent versions of this book. If you find any errata, please report them by visiting http://www.packtpub.com/support, selecting your book, clicking on the **errata submission form** link, and entering the details of your errata. Once your errata are verified, your submission will be accepted and the errata will be uploaded to our website, or added to any list of existing errata, under the Errata section of that title.

Piracy

Piracy of copyright material on the Internet is an ongoing problem across all media. At Packt, we take the protection of our copyright and licenses very seriously. If you come across any illegal copies of our works, in any form, on the Internet, please provide us with the location address or website name immediately so that we can pursue a remedy.

Please contact us at copyright@packtpub.com with a link to the suspected pirated material.

We appreciate your help in protecting our authors, and our ability to bring you valuable content.

Questions

You can contact us at questions@packtpub.com if you are having a problem with any aspect of the book, and we will do our best to address it.

1
Getting Started on UDK with iOS

So now it begins! Within just a few short pages you will take your first few steps towards becoming an iOS developer with UDK. But before we dive in head first, let's take a moment to learn just how UDK came to be in the first place and get everything set up to make your experience the best that it can be.

In this chapter we will:

◆ Learn about the Unreal Engine and what we expect to create

◆ Install UDK on our computer

◆ Go through an overview of UDK's directories

◆ Download and install UDK Remote

◆ Match the Mobile Previewer settings with your iOS device

◆ Describe the project we are going to be creating

Now that we have a firm grounding in what it is that we need as well as an overview of what the whole book is about, let's get started with the first thing we need to do, installing the program.

This first chapter is dedicated to offering a brief overview, from a beginner's point of view, of the exciting world that is UDK development for iOS.

During this chapter, we will be covering exactly what UDK is and how it came to enjoy its current popularity, including its evolution from prior versions of Epic Games' proprietary games development software.

Additionally, we'll be looking at what not to expect if you complete all the work showcased in this book. If you think you will be developing the next *Gears of War* game on your phone, for example, then I am afraid you're in for a bit of a surprise!

We will also be looking at how to install and run UDK on your machine and then make certain you are ready for iOS development. A key part of this is the Unreal Remote/Mobile Previewer functionality UDK offers, which we will be looking at in all its illustrated detail in this very chapter.

Finally, we'll be looking at the basic concept of the prototype game we will develop called Urban Warrior, which, yes, as mentioned previously, is not the next *Gears Of War* sequel, but at the same time will carry a lot of characteristics of a typical third-person shooter title which we all know and love!

Defining UDK

Unreal Development Kit (UDK) is a freely available version of Epic Games, a very popular Unreal game development engine.

First developed in 1998 to power the original Unreal game, the engine (which is C++ based) has gone from strength to strength, and has not only formed the backbone of household-name Epic Games titles, such as the very popular *Gears Of War* series, but has also been very successfully licensed out to third-party developers. Consequent titles range from *Batman: Arkham City* to *Mass Effect 3*, many of which are as equally successful as the games developed by its parent company.

Currently, the Unreal engine itself is in its fourth iteration and is considered to be a top of the range visualization tool. It is not only used in the gaming industry, but has also been used for doing any kind of work that demands real-time computer graphics. UDK uses Unreal Engine 3, but it is still a powerhouse in itself and is quite capable of delivering amazing experiences on iOS software.

The offering of UDK as a concept has evolved from Epic Games content generation tools very early on with Unreal titles; tools which proved to spawn a very healthy and thriving modification (modding) community. Originally, tools like these, such as UnrealEd (the editor tool with which a user can create their own in-game level), were available to anyone who bought the game.

In 2009, however, Epic turned that logic on its head by making their tools available to anybody, whether they owned an Unreal game or not. This proved to be a very successful move which expanded the Unreal developer user base thoroughly.

More recently Epic Games, as part of their constant and persistent updates of UDK, have added iOS functionality (in 2010), making sure that UDK can provide games for the ever-expanding mobile customer base that the iPhone/iPad/iPod Touch devices by Apple introduced. This was first demonstrated to the public by a live tech demo called *Epic Citadel*; a freely available download on the iTunes store which played like an interactive walkthrough of a medieval town. This attracted a record number of downloads as at that time it was truly groundbreaking to experience high quality real-time graphics on a mobile device. Take a look at the following screenshot:

In fact, although it is not within the scope of this book, very recently certain demos have surfaced highlighting a potential UDK / Adobe Flash Player pipeline, showcasing the very impressive penetration this games development application has made to a number of different platforms.

Of course, we are interested in iOS here, and we'll be covering that extensively in this book, starting from the bare basics and moving on to some more advanced concepts.

So what is it that we need to know about UDK and its mobile iOS limitations? Does it have any?

Don't expect to make Gears of War

Let's start with a fairly realistic statement; we can't make an AAA gaming title as seen on a contemporary console or PC, such as *Gears of War,* on iOS using UDK! It is a general limitation of doing mobile development using UDK.

The main reason for this is rather obvious; we just do not have access to the same hardware. The problem is not the software! UDK can deploy the same game on a PC or an iOS device, but it is the end-hardware specification that has the final say in what can be handled in real-time or not.

Mobile devices (and this of course includes iOS devices) have progressed by leaps and bounds over the last few years, and after many false starts mobile gaming today is a force to be reckoned with, both commercially and technologically. That still, however, does not change the fact that as an iOS UDK developer, you will work with more restricted hardware as opposed to, for example, someone developing for an Xbox 360 platform.

Let's look at this in more detail; these are some of the current iPhone 4S technical specifications:

♦ 960 x 640 pixel display

♦ 16 GB, 32 GB, or 64 GB Flash drive

♦ Dual-core 1 GHz Cortex-A9PowerVRSGX543MP2GPU

♦ 512 MB RAM

The newest iPad released in early 2012 has the following specifications:

♦ 2048 x 1056 pixel display

♦ 16 GB, 32 GB, or 64 GB Flash drive

♦ Quad-core PowerVRSGX543MP4GPU

♦ 1 GB RAM

While these specs are fairly impressive compared to both mobile devices of the past, and also the fact that we are talking about what is essentially a pocket gadget, they cannot really compare with the specification of a top-of-the-range gaming PC or even a current generation console.

This, of course, does not mean we can only develop poor or second rate games with UDK. Indeed, some of its contemporary examples highlight the huge potential it has in delivering AAA gaming experiences, even with its current limitations, borne, as described previously, from the hardware limitations of a mobile device.

The best example by far has got to be Chair Entertainment's and Epic Games' *Infinity Blade*, an epic third-person sword-fighting game which came out in late 2010 and is considered the ideal showcase for UDK's technical prowess on the Apple devices.

Already spawning sequels and with huge commercial success behind it from its iTunes Store business model, *Infinity Blade* was, and is, a big eye-opener for all aspiring games developers who want to use Unreal engine technology for a successful iOS title with a very modern feel and visuals.

To see just how powerful an iOS game can be, just look at the following screenshot for a fine example:

Downloading and installing UDK

We will download and install UDK on our computer for developing the games!

Time for action – installing UDK on your PC

UDK can be installed using following steps.

1. Start up your choice of Internet browser and visit UDK's website, `http://www.udk.com`. This is shown in the following screenshot:

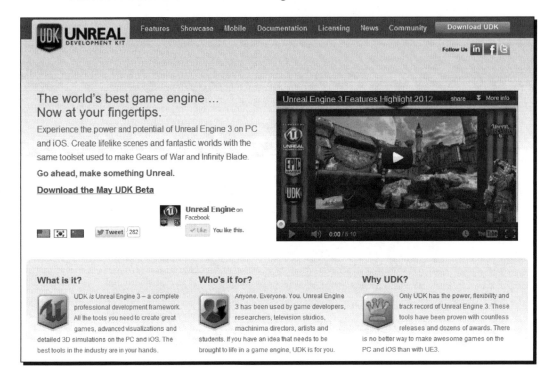

We will discuss how to download UDK in the next step, but for those just getting started with UDK, I would also urge you to take some time and explore this website further. It has a very thorough explanation of UDK and the features it has, regularly updated showcase projects (including commercially available games), information on licensing, and in short, it is a must-visit site (on a regular basis in fact) for any self-respecting UDK developer as here you can also find the latest up-to-date version of UDK for your use.

Epic Games also has a very active forum as a part of their community. For those tackling iOS development like we are, there are also community forums for us. You can find it by either hitting the **Community** tab at the top or then selecting **iOS Development** or just visit them directly at `http://forums.epicgames.com/forums/396-iOS-Development`.

2. Click on the blue **Download UDK** button on the top right-hand side corner of the page. This is shown in the following screenshot.

3. Download the latest release on the left-hand side by right-clicking on it and selecting **Save link as.....**.

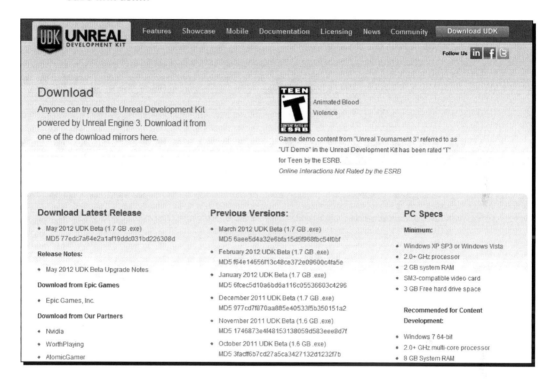

First of all, remember that you are now installing the full UDK application, not just the iOS-oriented one. There is in fact no such thing; UDK adopts a very holistic approach when it comes to multi-platform development.

Remember as well that Epic Games releases updates of UDK on a fairly regular basis.

However, as there can be incompatibility issues with older and newer versions, they have made every single update (its installer file) available with its release date clearly visible, from the very first one released (November 2009) to the current one (May 2012).

Please note that the May 2012 UDK Beta is the version we will be using in this book and while everything that we are doing in this book should work with later versions, UDK is constantly evolving and in months to come, there may be certain quirks in the engine that may not work until Epic will fix it in a later version.

4. It is likely that you will also get a prompt for a Microsoft .NET installation, please install that too. This shouldn't take as long as the UDK download (as you can see in the following screenshot).

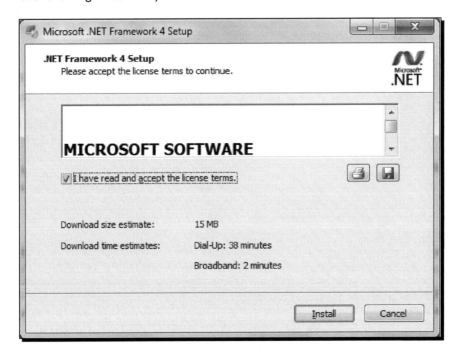

However, please note that this step may also trigger a restart of your PC, so save your work in any other applications beforehand.

5. Once the UDK installer has finished downloading, open the file and select to **Run** the file, if a security warning comes up allow the installer to make changes to your computer, if your computer asks.

6. The installer, at this point, will ask you to sign an **End User License Agreement** (**EULA**).To continue installing the program you have to agree to the terms by clicking on the **I Accept** button.

   Please be aware that Epic Games wants you to sign an end user license agreement at this stage.

   Typically, particularly for free applications downloaded from the Internet, people tend to disregard this bit and not read these in any great detail, and merely sign them by clicking on the **I Accept** button.

I would, however, strongly urge you to read this, particularly if you have aspirations towards becoming a professional UDK developer. You need to understand the agreement you are entering into for a number of reasons.

In general, using UDK for educational use or for non-profit reasons for the most part is completely free, but if you intend to charge for your game or make revenue off of it for any reason, you will have to pay Epic $99 up front as well as a percentage of revenue after the game has made over $50,000. For more details on licensing, take a look at the section *Commercialization* in *Chapter 8, Publishing and Monetizing Your Game*.

7. Next, install the program to your directory of choice. I used the default location. The installation process typically take a few minutes to complete (remember the large file size of the executable file you downloaded!).

8. Upon installation, you will have the option to **Launch UDK**. Do so, we will be using it later in this chapter.

9. Go to the directory that you installed UDK in (the one you selected in step 6). The default directory is C:\UDK\UDK-2012-05, as shown in the following screenshot:

Name	Date modified	Type
Binaries	05/11/2011 12:03	File folder
Development	05/11/2011 00:04	File folder
Engine	05/11/2011 00:05	File folder
UDKGame	05/11/2011 00:15	File folder

What just happened?

You've now installed UDK on your computer and taken your first step towards UDK development.

UDK directory overview

Epic Games provides a number of example maps and files which are worth exploring (including mobile ones), before setting off on the development of your own game. Now that the software is installed, let's take a look at what exactly the directories we created are holding.

Binaries

The **Binaries** folder holds a number of executable files, including the main UDK program and tools for artists and animators. Besides the UDK executables, we probably won't be touching anything here, but I'll briefly go over what the other folders hold.

- ◆ **ActorX**: It includes plugins to export models from 3dsMax or Maya

- ◆ **FaceFXPlugins**: It has tools for character facial animations

- ◆ **GFx**: It has tools used with Flash to integrate Scaleform in your game for HUDs or other things

- ◆ **iPhone/Mac**: It contains Packager programs used to export your game to be published on either the iOS or Mac platforms, respectively. This will be discussed in detail (on the iOS side) in Chapter 8, *Publishing and Monetizing Your Game*

- ◆ **SpeedTreeModeler**: This is a very quick way to make nice-looking trees and vegetation for game levels

- ◆ **Win32/Win64**: It contains the 32-bit and 64-bit versions of UDK and all of the libraries needed to run it

Development

Development holds the UnrealScript files of different classes created for the game. We won't be looking at it in this book, but feel free to look there some time to get a feel for how the gameplay logic works. For those comfortable with coding, you should feel free to read and extend things that were already created, but it is incredibly important to mention that you should never alter Epic's code.

Engine

Engine is where the engine files, holding resources, and configuration files are located. We won't be touching them in this book, but of special note is the iPhone folder, which can be used to set specific iPhone functionality for your game.

UDKGame

UDKGame will include following directories:

- ◆ **Autosaves**: This folder does not exist yet, as we haven't used UDK yet, but when you are working on levels later, this folder will be created in order to create backups of files you are working on. This isn't a replacement for you saving your work yourself, but in case UDK unexpectedly shuts down, you may have a chance to recover most of the work you did.

◆ **Build**: This folder contains assets that are required for publishing on different platforms. Of note is the `iPhone` folder which contains Resources that we will be using later in the book such as music and graphics for the App Store.

◆ **Config**: This folder contains `.ini` files, which we can use to change how the game itself functions. While we won't be touching this in the book, we will be using knowledge contained in the files, such as the key bindings which are found in the `DefaultInput.ini` file.

◆ **Content**: This is the folder where all of the assets that we create will go into. The file organization doesn't matter too much, as long as it makes sense to you. As long as it's in here, UDK will be able to find it. If you go into the **UDKGame** folder, then in **Content | Maps | Mobile**, you will be able to find a number of iOS-intended levels, including the aforementioned *Epic Citadel*, but also a very cool version of one of their earliest games (recreated lovingly on UDK); *Jazz the Jackrabbit*. This was originally a 2D platform game and it is a great nod to Epic Games' history to see it remade with a modern tool like UDK.

◆ **Flash**: For those of you interested in integrating Scaleform into your projects, here are examples of files created just for that purpose. You will need to have Flash in order to open the files and they will not work unless you set it up correctly. For more information about that, check out `http://udn.epicgames.com/Three/SettingUpScaleformGFx.html`.

◆ **Localization**: This folder contains files for converting your game into other languages.

◆ **Logs**: UDK keeps a record of what happens while you run it, so if errors occur, you can see exactly what went wrong. Useful for debugging, but you shouldn't need it.

◆ **Movies**: Any cut scene movies that you would like to use would be placed here, if you were developing for PC/Mac. We will not be using this folder for iOS development or in this book at all for that matter.

◆ **Script**: All source code generated ends up here when it is compiled. As we don't have any coding in this book, it will not be of much use to us.

◆ **Splash**: This folder contains images that show up when the game is starting up, as well as links to the **Unreal Developer's Network (UDN)** and the Epic Forums.

Setting up for iOS development with UDK

Before we get your iPhone interacting with UDK, here are a few brief notes you should be aware of. We've looked at installing UDK on our PC, but what about the mobile device requirements?

While we will go into detail about deploying your game on the actual device with all the issues this entails in a subsequent step-by-step and illustrated chapter, there are still some very important initial topics that need clearing up in terms of becoming a UDK iOS developer.

First of all, the devices currently supported by Epic Games for UDK iOS games production, according to Epic Games, are the following:

◆ iPhone 3GS

◆ iPhone 4/4S

◆ iPad

◆ iPad2

◆ iPod Touch third generation (other than for 8GB capacity third generation devices)

◆ iPod Touch fourth generation

If you have an older iOS device, then unfortunately you won't be able to carry out UDK development for it. Also worth noting is that the iPad third generation currently works in UDK by using the iPad 2's system settings, and will most likely be fully supported with its own system settings by the time you have this book in your hands.

Additionally, you will need to be running iOS version 3.2 or higher on your device, plus iTunes installed on your PC in order to do UDK development. However, in order to publish your game to the iOS App Store, you will be required to use a Macintosh computer which we will be using in *Chapter 8, Publishing and Monetizing Your Game*.

If you can adhere to all of the given requirements, then we can move on with our development of this and subsequent chapters.

We will, however, come back to this area in the last couple of chapters to cover topics such as the Unreal Frontend and iOS provisioning which will be paramount in post-production to the game's deployment and its eventual distribution.

Walkthrough of Unreal Remote

So, with the practicalities out of the way, let's get our first taste of what it's like to develop for an iPhone with UDK!

The first foray we will be undertaking in this section and chapter will be a modest one indeed, but it is still a good showcase of the capabilities of iOS game development with the Unreal engine, particularly in terms of interacting with the player.

It uses two important concepts that we will be utilizing later on in this book; UDK Remote and the Mobile Previewer.

UDK Remote is an application designed by Epic Games to push, touch, and also tilt controls - essentially everything you need to control an iPhone or iPad game - from the mobile device onto your development machine (PC).

The Mobile Previewer is an option that can be triggered inside the main UDK executable, which can be used to run the mobile UDK game on your PC. It is created for minor testing in much the same way that playing in the editor itself is an option in the main UDK executable. Think of the option as an emulator of what your game may look like on a specific mobile device. The option is not an entirely perfect one though, remember that the graphics processing unit on the PC will be more powerful than your iOS device's which could result in it being much faster in rendering content. Some visual effects results may be different too, for example, anti-aliasing. A good idea would be to very occasionally deploy the game on the mobile device just to make sure you are not exceeding its technical capabilities and also that everything looks the way it is supposed to. We will learn how to do this in a later chapter.

Both of these applications (UDK Remote and Mobile Previewer) can work in conjunction - as we will see!

The example in this section will not work without both your PC and your iOS device being connected to a Wi-Fi network; it is not enough for the device to be connected on a 3G network. Please make sure your device has its Wi-Fi settings on and is on the same network otherwise the following example will not work.

The first two chapters of this book will be using an iPhone 3GS for examples, while the later chapters will be using an iPad 2.

Time for action – downloading and installing UDK Remote

1. Before you do anything else, fire up the UDK editor. Then, go to the iTunes Store, which, as an iOS user, you should be fairly familiar with by this stage. Type in udk remote, as shown in the following screenshot:

2. Click on the **Free** button to change it to say **Install**. Click on the button again to install the UDK Remote application on your iOS device.

   Epic Games has actually made this a free application too like UDK itself, so it will not cost you anything.

3. Sync your device with the new app. Make sure your iOS device is properly synced by disconnecting it and looking at the menus of your device till you find the application installed.

4. Start up the UDK Remote application by tapping on its icon. You will be prompted to fill in details about your machine.

   The only setting you need to change in order to get UDK Remote to work is typing in the IP address of your computer so that your iOS device can communicate with it. Let's leave the other ones as they are for now.

   You can, however, before we resolve the IP address issue, quickly click on the **Done** button on your iOS device to check out UDK Remote.

   You should now be taken to the UDK Remote runtime screen which as you can see is very basic.

   Of course, there is no way this could work without setting up a communication between this and a host machine (your computer), as you can see from the error message.

5. You can go back to the settings by clicking on the **i** button at the top right-hand side corner of the screenas shown in the following screenshot:

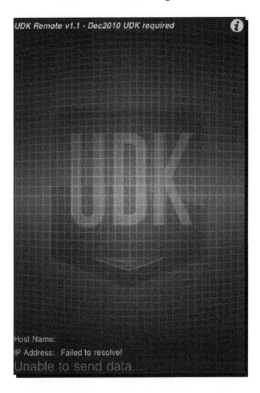

   So, 'what is my IP address?' you may ask. There is a quick way to find this out in case you do not know it.

6. On your computer, click on the **Start** menu and select **All Programs | Accessories | Command Prompt**, as shown in the following screenshot:

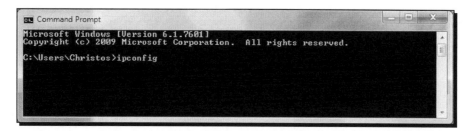

7. Type in `ipconfig` when you reach the command prompt and make a note of the IPv4 address that comes up. Go back to UDK Remote on your iPhone, click on **Computer Addr** and put in the value of the IPv4 address shown in the command prompt, and then click on the **OK** button to finish.

8. Go back to **Settings** on **UDK Remote** (as you can see you can interface the application with more than one computer) and click on **Done**.

9. Now, next to your IP address and port, you will see the following message, as shown in this screenshot:

[Waiting for connection...]

10. Your IP address and port will also be highlighted in yellow color as this means you have not hooked up with UDK yet, so let's do that next.

11. Open up the UDK editor that we launched in the previous section. Along the main toolbar, you will see an icon that looks like an iPhone with a play button next to it in the top-right corner. This is the **Play on Mobile Previewer** button.

12. Alternatively, you can also select **Build | Play on Mobile Previewer** from the top menu above it. This is shown in the following screenshot:

13. Wait till this fires up (it will take a few moments even for a very basic scene such as the default one) then look at your iPhone. The previously mentioned **Waiting for connection...** will have changed to **Connected to...** as shown in the following screenshot:

IP Address: Connected to

You will be prompted with the settings of UDK Remote (most of which are quite self-explanatory).

What just happened?

Look at your computer screen while dragging your finger(s) on your iPhone, you can now navigate around the basic UDK scene in a three dimensional space on your computer using your iPhone over the wireless network!

Use the multi-touch functionality to play around with this and get a feel for what you can do with the interactions provided.

The circular touch pad on the left-hand side, as shown in the following screenshot, can be used for movement while the one on right-hand side for strafing.

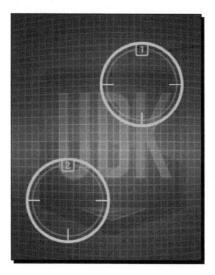

If you have played 3D games before, and, in particular, first-person shooters (not necessarily on an iOS platform either), this should be a very familiar way of controlling a player in a scene!

Spend some time experimenting with your first attempt at iOS game development!

Time for action – matching Mobile Previewer settings with your iOS device

Now that we have our interactions working between our iOS device and our PC, let's make sure that it is being created for the specific device that we are using. Thankfully, it's very simple to do that.

1. Before we move on, you should be aware that you can change some of the options on the Mobile Previewer, and indeed you should, in order to suit your device. Click on the **Edit mobile previewer settings** button as shown in the following screenshot:

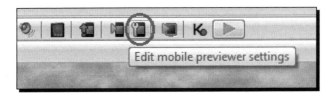

2. As in this chapter we are using an iPhone 3GS, I changed it to allow for that, you can also change the orientation of your display from landscape to portrait if you want. This really depends on the type of game you are developing.

Let's leave it on landscape. This is done as shown in the following screenshot:

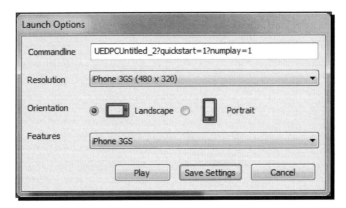

What just happened?

No matter which iOS device you have, you are now ready to use the UDK Remote and Mobile Previewer to test out all ideas and ultimately our prototype game in subsequent chapters, so already the step we have made towards this is a very important one!

Speaking of the prototype game, what exactly will we be developing?

Describing the concept of Urban Warrior, a third-person shooter title

We have talked about *Gears Of War* earlier and how difficult it would be to try to recreate it, with the same level of detail and complexity on an iOS device with UDK (which is based on the same engine, remember, that *Gears of War* was developed on).

How about we have a stab at that then and see how close we can get?

Rather than trying to produce a more casual, basic game with UDK, it would be of more interest to approach the work carried out in this book as small building blocks towards creating your own AAA title!

We have titled the game (tentatively and perhaps not particularly imaginatively) as **Urban Warrior** and it will have the following characteristics:

- ◆ It is a very typical single-player third-person shooter game, very much in the Gears of War style
- ◆ The playable 3D environment will be (mostly) a large open area of a city that will have interactive elements, such as doors that open when you walk up to them
- ◆ The player will traverse the game world getting involved in different scenarios depending on the path that he makes as he moves along towards his goal
- ◆ We will be creating our own custom AI system for enemies
- ◆ There will be custom assets of our own creation added into it to provide a unique experience for players

For now, despite being very broad, this brief is good enough for us to make a start on as we can begin exploring the very vast UDK functionality to accommodate some of the preceding goals and work our way towards some of the finer details of the game.

I will be returning to this key game idea throughout each subsequent chapter to discuss what progress we have made and, more importantly, how it is all fitting together into one cohesive gaming experience.

Pop quiz

Let's see if you can answer these questions, you should be able to answer all of these just by reading this first introductory chapter.

1. Which of the following iOS devices are NOT supported by UDK?

   a. iPad

   b. iPhone 2G

   c. iPad 2

   d. iPad (third Generation)

2. How do we find our IP address?

   a. It's already provided for us in the UDK Remote

   b. The IPv4 address that we got from the ipconfig output earlier

   c. Type in random numbers until it works

   d. Use the Command Prompt to use the Link-Local IPv6 address

3. Where and how can we find example/sample maps that Epic Games has provided us with on UDK?

   a. Epic doesn't provide examples

   b. Download them separately on the UDK website

   c. Look at tutorials on the Epic Game's Community Page

   d. They are located in the Content | Maps | Mobile folder of our UDK install

4. How do we make sure the Mobile Previewer is customized to our own iOS device or change the screen orientation for our iOS game?

   a. It is done automatically when we play the game by how it is held

   b. It is a setting on the UDK Remote app we set up

   c. It is found in the Edit mobile previewer settings

   d. We cannot change which device is used

Summary

Hopefully you've enjoyed taking the first few steps towards becoming an iOS games developer with UDK!

There's still plenty to do, but we have already managed to cover the following in this chapter:

- Learned about what UDK is
- Seen what can/cannot be achieved with UDK using an example
- Explored Epic Games' dedicated UDK website and download and install the application
- Downloaded and installed the UDK Remote
- An overview of what you will need to develop games with UDK on the iOS platform
- Interfaced your device with UDK on your PC and used it for basic interaction with Mobile Previewer
- Discussed the brief outline/concept of a basic, prototype game that we will be looking at in subsequent chapters

In the next chapter, we will delve deeper into using the UDK Editor (and doing a lot more than just playing with the UDK Remote and Mobile Previewer!), from learning about the basics of the interface of the application to adding the basic building blocks for your first shooter game.

2
Beginning Urban Warrior, a Third-person Shooter

At this point, we now have UDK installed and have gotten the UDK Remote to work so we are able to play our games on the PC using the input from our iOS device. This is a great start, but now it's time to get our hands dirty and start building something. In this chapter we will build upon what was covered in the first one by taking our first steps towards building our very first level.

In this chapter we shall:

◆ Learn about the UDK environment and the interface aspects of it that you will need to know

◆ Build brushes into our world to create an interior space

◆ Add textures, lighting, and 3D models in that space

So with that, let's get started!

Starting out

When beginning to use UDK, you may feel frustrated with how complex the editor looks at first glance or how it may not work the way you think it should. In order to help with the transition to these tools, we will ease into the process by looking at the basics of UDK, starting off with the key parts of its interface that you should know the existence of as we create our very first level!

A brief walkthrough of the UDK interface

Let us start by looking at the UDK interface, which is what you see upon starting the application and closing the welcome menu. While we brushed off learning what all of the menus and buttons did in the previous chapter, to just get the Mobile Previewer working, it is important to know all of the tools at your disposal, as one of the most important things a game developer can do is to know what tool to use to do a certain task. So you can make whatever you imagine appear on the screen.

To an extent, this will only really come with time, although I would definitely recommend exploring the interface and all the features shown in the screenshot by clicking on them and simply experimenting with them as much as possible (and not towards the end of an actual project), so that the basics of the interface eventually become second nature to you. I should also note that I will not cover all of the interface; some of it refers to advanced features that we don't need for now or won't be able to use due to our goal in creating an iOS game, though I will touch on some features not used briefly due to their importance in non-iOS games, should you want to do multi-platform development.

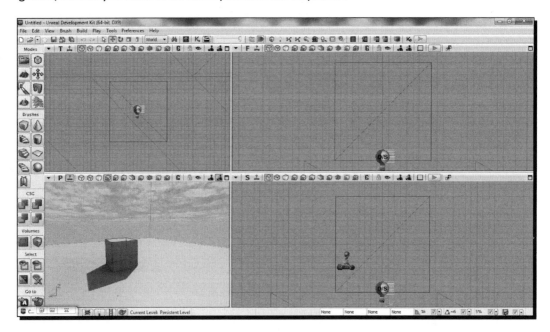

Toolbox sidebar

We will cover the icons you see on the far left-hand side to begin with. This is the toolbox categorized with **Modes**, **Brushes**, **CSG**, **Volumes**, **Select**, and **Go to** as labels above buttons that are associated with them. **Modes** are very important, so let us look at those first and foremost.

If you don't remember what something is, if you leave your mouse cursor on anything after a short period the icon's name/function will appear; this will be very handy for using the following guide and identifying the part of the interface you are on and what it does!

Modes

Modes contain all of the different ways of interfacing with your level. Specifically, it contains the following functions:

- ◆ **Camera Mode**: This is UDK's basic default camera mode. You will be working in this one quite a lot!

- ◆ **Geometry Mode**: This brings up the basic tools for editing geometry and in particular CSG brushes. (For manipulations similar in many ways to what you would do in an application, such as Autodesk's 3D Studio Max). One of the nice things it allows us to do is build objects to the grid making it easier to not get holes in our level. We will be using it extensively in *Chapter 6, Bringing It All Together*.

- ◆ **Terrain Editing Mode**: This mode is used for the creation of terrains.

- ◆ **Texture Alignment Mode**: This mode is used for aligning textures properly on brushes with operations such as rotation, among others.

- ◆ **Mesh Paint Mode**: This is an in-editor vertex color painting tool.

- ◆ **Static Mesh Mode**: This is a tool to assist with quick static mesh additions in a level (via speeding up their placement process). This is very useful if, for example, multiple static meshes are used to populate a scene.

- ◆ **Landscape Mode**: This landscape creation tool with abilities used in changing terrain allows you to import height map data if you are familiar with it. However, UDK on iOS systems does not support terrain, so we will not be using it.

- ◆ **Foliage Mode**: This is a semi-automatic tool for the creation of foliage.

Refer to the screenshot for these modes.

Brushes

Brushes are the geometry that we can bring into the world. The following are the possible options of things we can create, and we will discuss what the geometry really is and how it works after we discuss the interface. The following features are available in brushes:

♦ **Cube**: This is a cube/box-shaped brush builder

♦ **Cone**: This is a cone-shaped brush builder

♦ **Curved Staircase**: This is a curved staircase brush builder

♦ **Cylinder**: This is a cylinder-shaped brush builder

♦ **Linear Staircase**: This is a standard, straight staircase brush builder

♦ **Sheet**: This is a flat 2D plane-like brush builder (where subdivisions can also be added, if needed)

♦ **Spiral Staircase**: This is another curved staircase brush builder, this time however with no restrictions in the angle of the base used (the previous Curved Staircase one had a restriction of 360 degrees on this, hence the spiral name for this one rather than a curve)

♦ **Tetrahedron (Sphere)**: This is a sphere-like CSG brushes builder

♦ **Cards**: This is a brush builder which, because of its appearance, can be utilized for the creation of various special/visual effects with the use of textures such as low-cost trees by using two textures instead of a model

Refer to the screenshot for these options:

The next part of the toolbox contains the brush CSG operations (again, see the next section *Volumes and Select* for a more thorough explanation of the terms, suffice it to say these are key in shaping brushes into a meaningful and playable level):

- ◆ **Add**: This uses the last selection of the brush-builder mode, and with that, as a template, creates an additive brush in the level

- ◆ **Subtract**: This is used in the same way as the preceding option, but this time there is the creation of a subtractive brush

- ◆ **Intersect**: This will only show the section of a brush that overlaps other intersecting brushes with the rest not being visible

- ◆ **Deintersect**: This results in the inverse of the previous operation

These are shown in the following screenshot:

Volumes and Select

Volumes and **Select** cover the following features:

- ◆ **Add Special Brush**: This facilitates the creation of more complex brushes.

- ◆ **Add Volume**: In much the same way that clicking on a CSG operation will create a new brush, clicking on **Add Volume** will create a piece of geometry with a special property. Volumes are invisible, but can be used for all sorts of effects like creating water, lava, or triggering different events. Feel free to play around and see all of the kinds of things you can do. We will be using many different kinds of volumes in this book.

- ◆ **Show Selected Only**: This is useful (as with the other three selection buttons) in order to make selections in a busy and/or cluttered level; this is a tool for displaying exclusively the selected actors in your editor/game level.

- ◆ **Hide Selected**: This is a tool for hiding the selected actors in your level (the reverse of the preceding function).

- ◆ **Invert Selection**: This is a tool for inverting the previous actions.

- ◆ **Show All**: This is a reset tool for the actions of selecting where all actors are now displayed in the editor again.

Refer to the screenshot for these features:

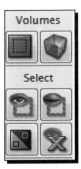

Go to and Builder Brush

Finally, we have **Go to** (**Actor** and **Builder Brush**) which, like the previous ones, are selection tools to assist with reverting to either an actor or the brush in your viewport. Again, these can be very handy and useful, maybe not so much with what we are doing in this chapter (as you would be hard pressed to lose your builder brush in a level consisting of one room!) but as soon as your game starts expanding, you will find that you will be using them more and more in order to save time looking through your increasingly complex UDK editor structures. The following screenshot shows this tool:

Viewport toolbar

Now let's look at the **Viewport** toolbar. Each of the viewports that you are currently using has a set of icons above them which we refer to as the Viewport toolbar. By default, UDK uses four viewports like most 3D modeling programs. However, there are other options which we will be talking about in *Chapter 5, Action Sequences for Urban Warrior*.

We have the following viewports from left-hand side to right-hand side:

- **Viewport Options**: This makes a number of options available to you, for example, showing frames per second within the viewport. It should be noted that many can be switched on and off (like the aforementioned one, for example) but are also available as icons (discussed as follows).
- **Viewport Type**: You can switch between **Perspective**, **Top**, **Front**, and **Side**.

- **Real Time**: This will show what the game will look like at runtime, turning on sound effects and particle systems. This does however have an effect on editor speed and performance so it is to be used sparingly and/or only when necessary.

- The next 11 icons from **Brush Wireframe** to **Lighting Only with Texel Density** switch the various views in the viewport to whichever one required by the user.

- **Game View**: This showcases the visualization that would be seen in runtime (for example, click on the default Perspective Viewport to see all wireframes disappear).

- **Lock Viewport**: This is self-explanatory to an extent but will lock not the viewport itself, but the **Go to** actions described previously.

- **Lock Selected Actors to Camera**: This will "lock" the next actor selection (after the button/icon is clicked) to the viewport camera. You can then move the camera and click this again and the actor will also be moved. This is essentially a handy tool for moving parts of the level/game in the viewport in a very rapid manner.

- **Level Streaming Volume Previs and Post Process Volume Previs**: This will enable streaming and post-processing manipulations to be visualized in the given/selected viewport. Post-processing doesn't work inside UDK on an iOS device, and as we are not using multiple levels, we have no need to use Level Steaming Volume, so we will not be using these.

- **Camera Movement Speed**: This will allow you to change the viewport camera speed (four settings/different speeds provided).

- **Play In Viewport**: This will allow you to play the game in the viewport, which is very handy for prototyping, but will not be representative of your game on iOS.

- **Tear Off Floating Copy**: This will undock/detach the given viewport from the four-viewport mode.

- **Maximize Viewport**: This will maximize a viewport (temporarily eliminating the four-viewport mode) and, when clicked again, revert back to the original, which is very handy for quickly zooming in on an area or specific perspective.

Refer to the screenshot for these options:

The toolbar

Now let's move to the top of the screen, right below the main menu bar and explore all the icons found inside the toolbar:

- **Create New Level**: This will create a new level, not however before UDK asks you to save your current one
- **Open An Existing File**: This will load a level which is saved; again same prompt as the preceding one applies
- **Dropdown menu**: This is a feature for finding recently accessed levels
- **Toggle Map File As Favorite**: This is a way of signifying a UDK level as a favorite one
- **Save Current Level**: This will save your level
- **Save All Levels**: This will save multiple levels
- **Save All Writable Packages**: This will save packages
- **Undo...**: This is fairly self-explanatory, do remember however that after a **Build...** process for a level this will not work
- **Redo...**: The same rule as the preceding one applies!
- **Selection Mode**: This is a tool to only select and not manipulate in any way the parts of the level
- **Translation Mode**: This is a tool to move parts of the level
- **Rotation Mode**: This is a tool to rotate parts of the level
- **Scaling Mode**: This is a tool to scale parts of the level uniformly, in the X, Y, and Z axes?combined
- **Non-Uniform Scaling Mode**: This is a tool to scale parts of the level non-uniformly, such as stretching it, for example, in one specific axis rather than all three
- **Reference Coordinate System**: World and local spaces apply here (the two available modes) as the coordinate systems affecting transformations
- **Find Actors**: This is a useful tool for locating actors in more complex levels containing many different actors
- **Open The Content Browser**: This opens the asset repository window for UDK; we will be looking at this later in this chapter
- **Open Unreal Kismet**: This opens Unreal Kismet which is the UDK visual-scripting tool for scripted events, sequences, and other complex tasks
- **Open Unreal Matinee**: This opens Unreal Matinee which is the way that UDK creates cinematic scenes as well as a number of other things that involve directed movement

Refer to the following screenshot:

Continuing along the toolbar, we have the following options:

- **Distance to far clipping plane**: This is a far clipping plane slider, used typically for performance savings

- **Allow Translucent Selection**: This is an icon which helps in the selection of the translucent parts of the UDK level/game

- **Encompass To Select**: This is a self-explanatory selection tool

- **Low Quality Materials**: This allows the user to display low quality materials on objects for those allowing it

- **Build Geometry For Visible Levels**: This creates the level geometry for the level you are working on

- **Build Lighting**: This creates the lighting for the level you are working on

- **Build Paths**: This creates the paths for the level you are working on

- **Build Cover Nodes**: This creates the cover nodes for the level you are working on

- **Build All**: This creates all of the above. Typically, when you work on your level, you don't have to use this option every time you make a small change to see what the game is like when played. That being said, do remember you cannot undo something being built. Remember as well that for larger levels, if you are working on lighting only and want to update your map, you do not have to build everything, but merely use the aforementioned button

- **Build All and Submit to Source Control**: This will build everything and also use version control, useful for tracking particularly for larger/team-based projects. However, this is not set up as a default option

- **Lighting Quality Setting**: These are settings for lighting; the ones available are preview, medium, high, and production

- **Fullscreen Mode**: This switches the editor itself to full screen mode

- **Toggle Real Time Audio**: This is the in-editor audio button, the volume for this can be adjusted by right-clicking and using the resulting slider

- **Emulate Mobile Features**: This is used for rendering emulation changing to a mobile one for a better approximation of the resulting outcome on a mobile device (graphics-wise)

- **Install on iOS device**: This is self-explanatory and a button we will be using in *Chapter 8, Publishing and Monetizing Your Game*

- ◆ **Mobile Previewer**: We have already used this so you should know what it does! Needless to say we will be using more of it too

- ◆ **Edit Mobile Previewer Settings**: We have also used this already so you should know what this does too

- ◆ **Start this level on PC**: This launches PC run-time of the game/level, but as we are purely doing iOS development, we will not be using it as it does not emulate mobile input or use the OpenGL renderer used to simulate mobile rendering

- ◆ **Enable Kismet Debugging**: This can be switched on and off and helps with the Kismet sequence debugging

- ◆ **Play this level in an editor window**: This is self explanatory and very useful again for rapid prototyping, but it is not representative of what an iOS device will be able to do

Refer to the following screenshot:

Exploring the main menu bar

Now let us move on to the main toolbar at the top of the screen. I will run through this in a quicker fashion as opposed to the previous features since the majority of the functions are replicated (we have already covered them and they are duplicated in different parts of the toolbar menus) and some of these are more advanced and I would like to avoid overcomplicating the first few steps in UDK that we are making in this chapter. It is still however worth quickly looking through these as there are many useful options here too.

These are the main menu bar options:

File

Like most programs, under the **File** menu you will be able to open files, save them, and create new ones. You have the opportunity to import files into your level or export your level into a file as well. The bottom of the menu allows you to easily select your favorite levels as well as those you've recently opened.

Note that **Save** does not have a shortcut in UDK and by clicking *Ctrl+S* you are actually creating a subtractive brush. Be sure that you save your levels by selecting **File | Save**.

Edit

This is the location of the normal **Undo/Redo** functionality that programs usually have as well as an additional way to access things we discussed before like the ability to **Translate**, **Rotate**, and **Scale** objects. You also have access to **Cut**, **Copy**, **Paste**, **Duplicate**, and **Delete** functionality of objects inside your level. The bottom section allows for different ways to select different objects' of note is **Find Actors** which will bring you to a menu showing you everything in your level, making it easy to find something specific you're looking for.

View

The **View** menu offers the ability to see all of the windows available inside of UDK. All of the different types of browser windows can be accessed as well as the properties of an actor, surface, or the level itself. You can adjust the properties of snapping that the level does in how far you can drag, scale, and rotate an object. There are options to customize your own UDK interface as well, such as changing your viewports or toggling the use of full screen mode.

Brush

The **Brush** menu contains all of the things that we discussed previously with the toolbox sidebar with the additional option to import or export the different brushes that you create.

Build

The **Build** drop-down menu contains various options in terms of rebuilding your levels. The menu also allows you to only build the things that you've changed, making it run quicker; you don't want to rebuild your lighting every time unless you've changed something after all, as it normally takes a long time with a larger level.

Play

The **Play** section of the main menu bar gives you the option to play your game in different ways based on the platform you are creating for. We will be using the On Mobile Previewer for most of the book, but we will show how to install on iOS devices in *Chapter 8, Publishing and Monetizing Your Game*.

Tools

The **Tools** menu, however, does seem to have a lot of exclusive (non-icon) content, such as the ability to check a map of errors (compile it without actually building it), cleaning up BSP and others, although most of these are not of immediate interest to us for the time being as they do not significantly impact the beginner's path to creating a basic game. All these options are shown in the following screenshot:

File   Edit   View   Brush   Build   Play   Tools   Preferences   Help

Preferences

The **Preferences** toolbar, which is the longest toolbar, has many different options which can toggle on or off to customize your UDK experience. It is also worth noting that a lot of people starting out will often check or uncheck something here, often by using a keyboard shortcut or by mistake, and then be very perplexed when something does not work right or is not visible! For that reason, it is worth knowing about the options so you can try to solve the problem by yourself. The following screenshot shows us the options available in preferences:

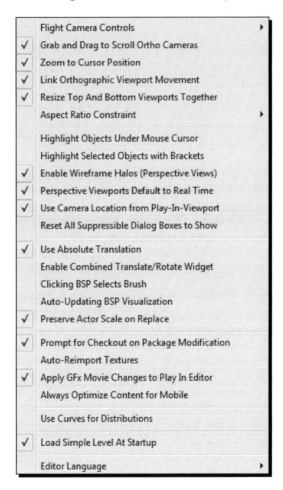

Help

Finally, **Help** carries information about online help, forums, the version of Unreal being used, startup tips, and Swarm-UDK's distribution solution for multi-core computers (which can help with speeding up lighting calculations).

The console bar

To finish with our look at the interface, let's finally focus at the bottom of the screen at what is known as the **console bar**. Refer to the following screenshot:

At this part, there is a command line in which you can input console commands directly into the Unreal Editor. We will be using console commands later in the book, but inside the actual game and not the editor, but the option exists.

In addition, there is a **Source Control** icon (which is not set up by default), a lighting and paths build status button and a package icon.

Moving towards the bottom right of this part of the UDK editor, you can also get information on your mouse cursor position (coordinates) and, if you have an object selected, information about the object itself.

Additionally, you can perform manual operations on items using the four DrawScale textboxes (**DrawScale** plus **DrawScale3D X**, **DrawScale3D Y**, and **DrawScale3D Z**). There are the Drag, Rotation, and Scale Grids as well that are something incredibly important to have turned on when creating your level. With the option is disabled, when an item is translated it can be moved to any position causing holes. For example, if you are trying to create a door by using a subtractive brush being placed over an additive one, if the brushes are off by just a tiny bit the section that is not covered by the brush will form a wall. When building our actual game level we will be using this to great effect.

Finally, auto-save features are also found here which will automatically save the map to a backup file in case Unreal crashes and/or breaks your level. Better to be safe than sorry! The following screenshot shows all these settings:

Keyboard shortcuts

One final note; keyboard shortcuts.

UDK, as with all 3D design applications makes extensive use of these (as you have seen from screenshots already) and you can use your keyboard to your heart's content here. One piece of advice however; if you use other 3D applications (or indeed ANY applications with shortcuts), be aware because UDK is a complex tool and you may, as I mentioned earlier, initiate something by mistake or change a setting you did not want to change simply because you did not remember the right keyboard shortcut at the time.

This happens to the best of us, but it would be best to avoid it if we can.

That being said, as the book continues on in addition to showing how to access things from menus, I will introduce the shortcuts that I personally use on a common basis while working with the tool.

Creating environments and the basics of level design

Before we delve into utilizing the interface described previously and also putting to use the knowledge gained so far for the creation of an interactive level, (your first one!) let us delve into some theory.

CSG brushes

We've been throwing around the word brushes and CSG a lot, so it's a good idea to define what that actually is. **Constructive Solid Geometry (CSG)** is a term used in UDK for world geometry which UDK creates from the brushes that you create in the level. Brushes, on the other hand, are three-dimensional objects that are used to define space. We define that space in four different ways: **Add**, **Subtract**, **Intersect**, and **Deintersect**.

Static meshes

Static meshes, on the other hand, are polygonal creations that can also be used for the formation of a game level in Unreal/UDK which are not moving within the world, but don't worry, we'll also cover how to create moving objects as well in a future chapter. In this chapter, we will be placing meshes to give our environment something other than walls to see.

Later in this book, we will be looking at importing static meshes into UDK from a 3D modeling package, thus showcasing the limitless potential of world creation and world mesh population of the engine, given some basic 3D asset creation skills from the developer.

The differences between CSG brushes and static meshes

So what are the differences then between using brushes and/or static meshes? Why use one or the other?

You should be aware that today static meshes are really the professional's choice in world creation in UDK, for two simple reasons: performance and aesthetics. It is much faster to use static meshes and (provided you use quality ones!) they will look much, much better than brushes. Brushes have also had or led to their fair share of problems such as causing holes, and static meshes have provided the much needed solution to resolving such inefficiencies.

However, there is still a place for brushes. In the game industry, many game designers will block out a level using brushes and get the scripting working correctly. That way the designer is able to focus on making the game fun and making sure the functionality of the level is completed to make sure that everything will work. We will be using this mindset for this chapter and in the next chapters up to *Chapter 6, Bringing It All Together*. With the level completed, a level designer can then give the level to an environmental artist who will then replace the brushes with meshes that they've created, which is what we will be doing in *Chapter 7, Advanced Content Creation for Urban Warrior*. That being said, all studios are different, so a workflow in one company could be completely different to another's.

Moving around viewports

Clicking inside of a viewport will give you access to the camera that it has. During the course of the book, we will work in a variety of viewports so you will be using the following to navigate efficiently in the level:

- Holding the **Left Mouse Button** (**LMB**) while moving left or right will rotate your camera left and right, while moving up and down will move forward and backwards along the camera's X-axis

- For looking around, use the **Right Mouse Button** (**RMB**)

- A combination of the LMB and RMB will result in your camera panning up and down its Z-axis or left-hand side and right-hand side along the Y-axis

The mouse scroll wheel will pan along the camera's X-axis giving the appearance of zooming in and out.

Adding world geometry and texturing to the game

Now that we have all of the groundwork covered, let's get started on making our very own first level from scratch!

Time for action – creating a basic room

1. To begin with, under **File** select **New** and from the popup that comes up, select the **Blank Map** option. At that point, you should see something similar to what is shown in the following screenshot:

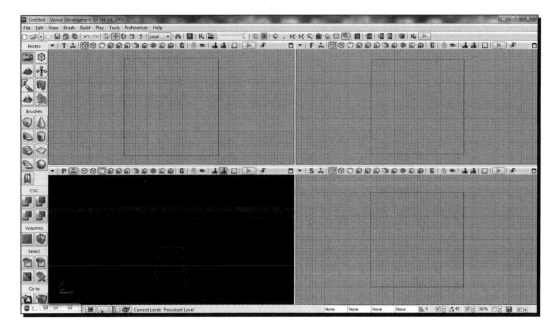

2. Right-click on the **Cube** brush to bring up the **Brush Builder** dialog box. Change the settings in the pop-up window as shown in the following screenshot (in the section **X** fill 1024, in the section **Y** type 512, and in the section **Z** fill 16). Click on **Build** and **Close**. Your builder brush has the size you want now!

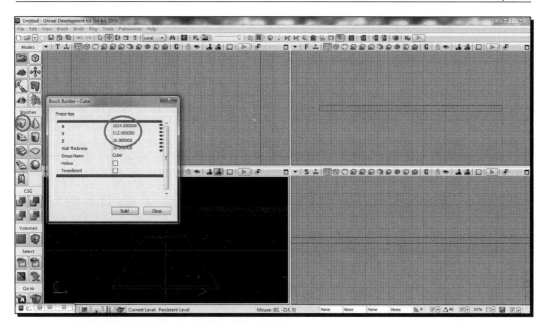

3. Click on the **CSG Add** operation icon which is located on the side toolbar, underneath the **CSG** option. You should see your first piece of geometry created.

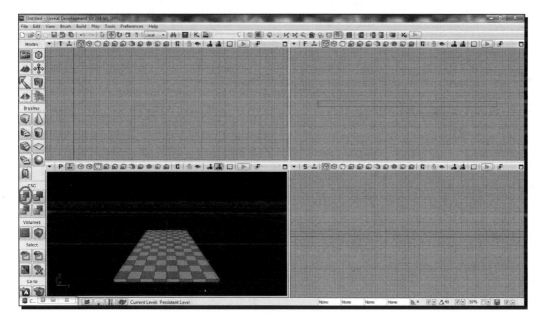

4. Left-click on the builder brush to select the object. You should see three arrows somewhere along the builder brush, facing each of the different axes with their own color. This is referred to as the **widget**, but if it looks like each of the axes are arrows, then it is in **Translation** mode. If it does not look like that, press the *Space bar* until it looks like it does in the following screenshot. With the **Translation** tool, set to translate, drag the brush upwards, and click on the **CSG Add** button again. As we are just showing the tool, don't worry so much about the height, but try to match the screenshot. You now have your ceiling geometry. You may at this stage want to start maximizing viewports (the **Perspective** in this case) back and forth to get a better view of what you're doing.

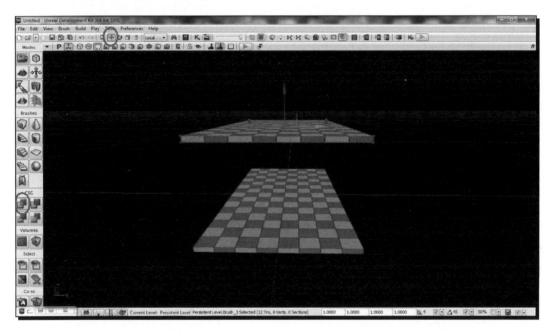

5. With the **Builder Brush** selected, click on the **Rotation** icon (or press *Space* until you see the tool in the next screenshot) and rotate through -90 degrees in the **Front** viewport in the appropriate axis, till you get the result as shown in the following screenshot:

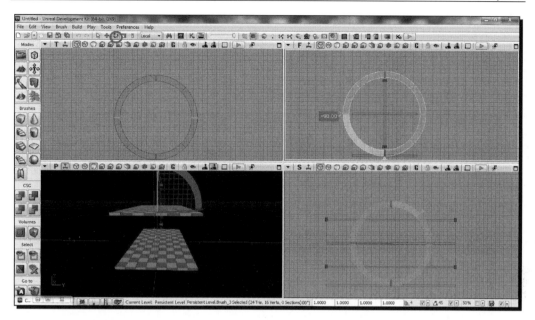

6. Move this into place as the left-hand side wall and then non-uniformly scale it in the right axis to squash it into place. This is important; this now needs to perfectly match up. It is at this point that you will have to start making use of the **Drag**, **Rotation,** and **Scale Grid** snapping tools at the bottom right-hand side which we talked about previously. Refer to the following screenshot:

These will snap your transformations into the grid whether it is moving, rotating, or scaling, thus giving you a more accurate way of placing geometry in exact places.

It really is important for these to snap nicely and in a clean manner, as this is a practice you need to get used to. Make sure that your first two pieces (ceiling and floor) are also nicely snapped, as well as the newly created side wall.

It will take some practice for you to find the right settings for this and very often you will have to change your snapping settings depending on what you are doing (and viewport you are in) so you need to get accustomed to this now.

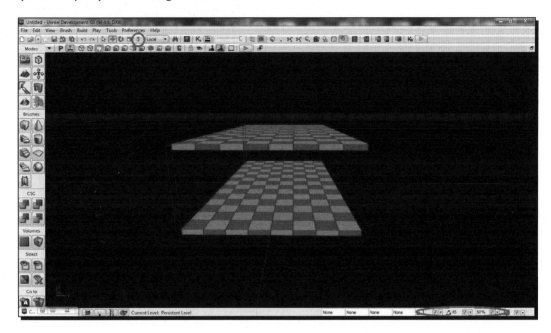

7. Use **CSG Add** once more on the left-hand side wall, then follow this process for the right-hand side wall, the front, and back walls to create an enclosed room.

This is similar to what we have been doing so far and should pose no issues.

You are now slowly getting used to using the **Builder Brush**, moving, rotational and scaling transformations, **CSG Add** operations and the snap tools.

Remember to work in all viewports to make sure that what you are doing translates well in a three dimensional space and snaps properly to the grid!

Once you have done the right-hand side wall and the front and back ones, you should end up with the same result as shown in the following screenshot, all cleanly snapped to the grid and to each other.

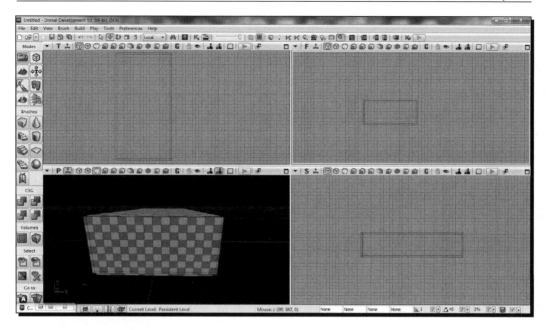

What just happened?

We have now completed our first room inside of UDK! It may not look like much right now, but we are going to fix that quite soon.

This is now your room and at this point we are done with brushes for this chapter, but we shall return to using them in the next one. There is one more thing to do before we move on. The room that we created is enclosed but it is actually hollow and we should be able to fit in it. To do so, hold down the left mouse button (LMB) and move it forward in order to move forward, and hold both LMB + RMB to move down and up, in order to position yourself inside the space you just created to admire it.

Now this looks okay, but I'd say it's missing something in order to really make it realistic. the walls are all the same! Thankfully, we can use textures to make the walls come to life in a very simple way, bringing us one step closer to that AAA quality.

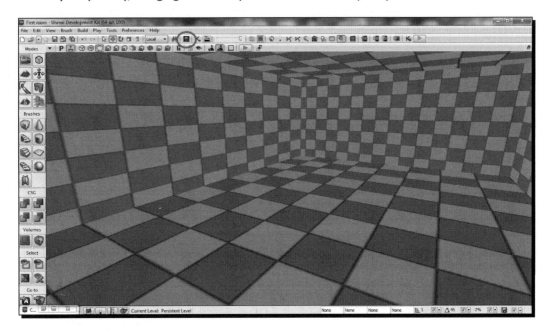

Time to apply some textures.

Time for action – texturing the level

1. Select all side walls (I have three as shown in the previous screenshot, make sure you select the one in the back too) by left-clicking on them while holding down the *Ctrl* key and then maximize your **Content Browser** (this is something which opens by default when you run UDK and I had minimized. If you had closed it, then hit the icon indicated in the next screenshot).

   The **Content Browser** is UDK's asset repository interface.

   We will be making extensive use of that for many actions but for now let us just go over a basic process so that we pick three different existing textures that we can use in our scene.

2. Type brick into the **Search** textbox at the top of the **Content Browser**. To help demonstrate what I mean, this is highlighted in the next screenshot:

3. Left-click and select **M_NEC_Walls_BSP_Brick1** from the results and click on **Fully Load** from the menu that appears (as shown in the next screenshot). Then minimize the **Content Browser** as we now want to apply our textures.

4. Right-click anywhere on the selected wall surface (it needs to be there, however, and not on one of the other unselected walls). On the menu that appears, select **Apply Material:M_NEC_Walls_BSP_Brick1**.

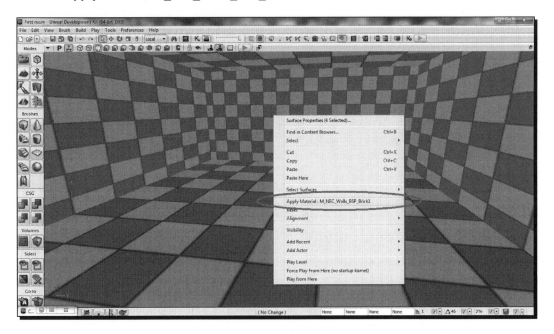

We have just textured our first piece of geometry in UDK!

We will be making one slight manipulation on that, but first let us do the ceiling and floor too.

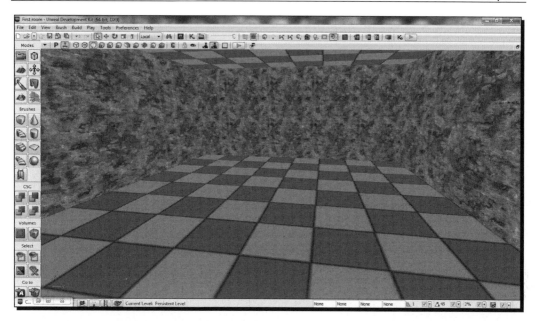

5. Use the **Content Browser** and the same process, but for the ceiling pick **M_NEC_ Ceilings_SM_TURK182** (after typing `ceiling` in the command line) and for the floor **M_ASC_Floor_BSP_Tile01** (after typing `floor` in the command line).

You will see the next screenshot:

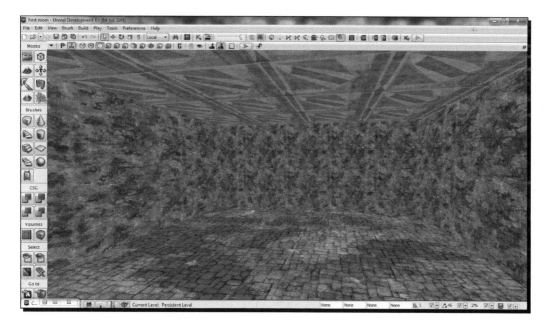

This looks OK (and a lot better than what we had before) but many subtle manipulations can be made to make it look even better. One possible option is to tile (multiply) textures further in a certain area. This is so that the proportions, according to the size of the room, become more realistic rather than skewed (which can spoil the illusion of any virtual world in a game). You will be doing quite a lot of this for your own games/levels.

6. Select all the side walls again in the same way as before and right-click on them. You will see the menu shown in the following screenshot:

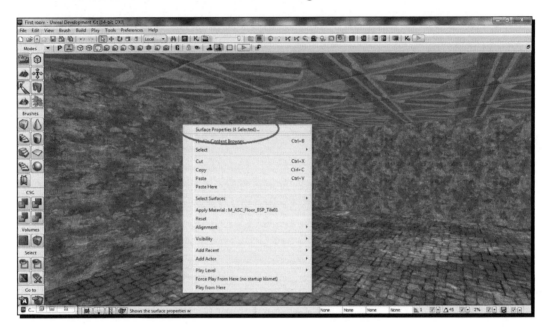

7. Select **Surface Properties(4 Selected)...** and on the resulting window change **UTile** and **VTile** to 3 and 3 and then click on **Apply**. This is shown in the following screenshot:

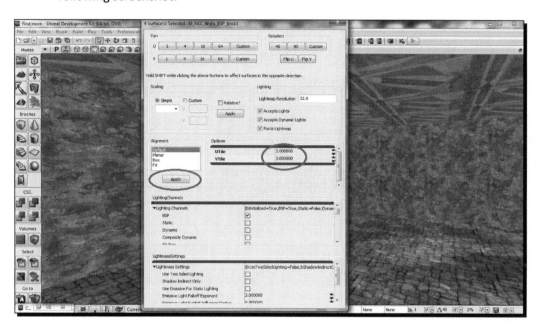

What just happened?

We have now taken our first step towards game level creation in UDK. We now have a room that looks like it could in fact be a room, complete with proper walls being applied to it. Now that we have a room that's worth looking at, let's get the last few steps completed so we can see it in our game!

Creating lighting for the game

Point lights are the simplest type of lights that can be added. They are the lights that spread light evenly in all directions, and can be used to illuminate the scene quickly, particularly for prototyping purposes.

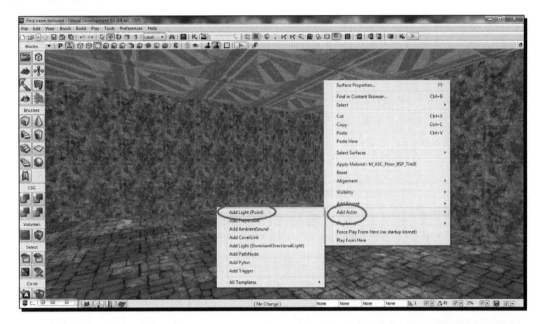

Time for action – lighting the level

However, at this point if we play the game, we will only see pitch black. This is due to no lights existing in the game. Let's put them in now!

1. Right-click towards the ceiling of the level in the **Perspective** viewport, where you should still be, and then go to **Add Actor | Add Light (Point)**. You will see something similar to the next screenshot:

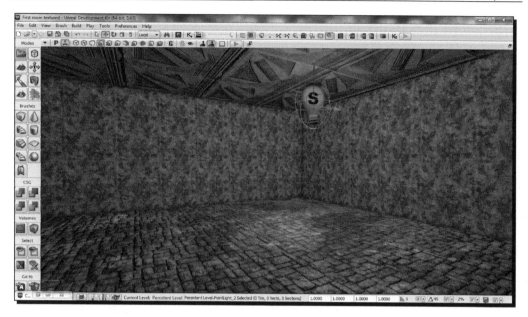

As you can see, the light has been added and the illumination in the scene has changed (you may want to move it downwards a bit, by the way, if it intersects with the ceiling).

2. Switch back to a four-viewport view and position this approximately in the middle of our scene (at the top viewport) as shown in the following screenshot:

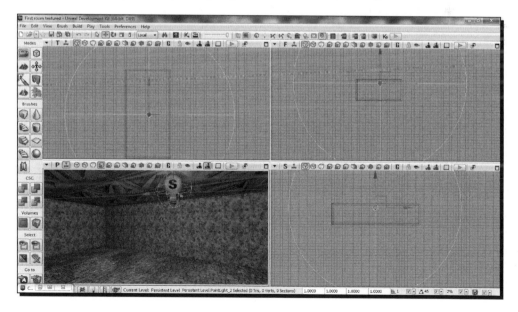

3. Double left-click on the light in any viewport. This will bring up the object properties menu. In the window that comes up, you will get the **Light Properties** section. In that section, set the value of **Radius** to 512 and **Brightness** to 2.

This will give a bright middle area and darker areas around the opposing front and back walls (for a more atmospheric look).

Other settings can be changed, but for now this should be enough to get a first taste of illuminating a scene.

4. It is now time to check out what this looks like in run-time. Before we do that, UDK would like to know where the player starts from (otherwise we cannot proceed to run time).()Right-click in the middle of the room (approximately anyway) in the **Perspective** viewport and select **Add Actor | Add Player Start**.

We now need to build this in order to see it in run time.

5. Go to **Build | Build All**. Depending on your hardware this may take a short while.

6. When this finishes, click on the **Mobile Previewer** icon. You should see our level come up.

You can move around by using the *W, A, S,* and *D* keys or by clicking on the two joysticks that have come up on the screen. If you would like to, you can use your iOS device to navigate around the scene using the UDK Remote that we set up in the previous chapter. This is shown in the following screenshot:

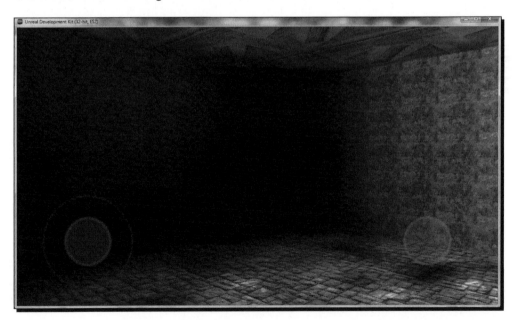

What just happened?

Congratulations! We have completed a very basic first game level with UDK from scratch that can run on an iOS device!

Creating actors and static meshes for the game

To wrap up the tasks worked on for this chapter, let us look at enriching the level with static meshes (static mesh actors have additional properties, from animations to sound and physics). The process of adding a basic static mesh as opposed to adding one with additional properties, however, is identical and we will start with this so we get accustomed to the fundamentals first.

Time for action – adding static mesh detail

1. Go back to the **Content Browser** again and type `barrel` in the **Search** line. This is shown in the following screenshot:

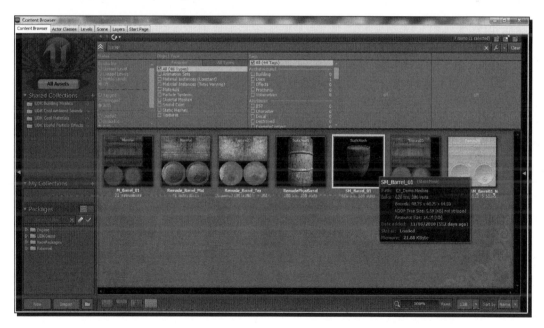

2. Make sure you right-click and **Fully Load** the barrel we will use (in this case **SM_Barrel_01**).

3. Go back to your level and right-click anywhere on the floor. With the floor selected, right-click and select **Add StaticMesh:E3_Demo_Meshes_SM_Barrel_01**.

   Notice that this can be added a variety of other ways; refer to my explanation of this at the beginning of this section.

4. Double click on the barrel or press *F4* to bring up the **Object Properties** and change the **Draw Scale** value to **0.7**.

This is only one example of a way to scale an object. You can also scale them using the usual icon transformations we used with the walls or with the **Draw Scale 3D** values seen in **Properties**. There are many ways to accomplish the same thing in UDK. This step is shown in the following screenshot:

What just happened?

The barrel can now be seen in the level. You have your first static mesh in there, but more can be done with this concept, especially now that you have mastered the first one.

Have a go hero – adding multiple static meshes for extra detail

Now try and be creative! Add a few of these in different parts of the room. Try and keep a random look in their structure of appearance. Select **Edit | Duplicate** (or *Ctrl + D*), then move and rotate into place.

You will see something similar to the following screenshot:

You have the skills at this stage to start experimenting with adding other static meshes/actors to enrich the scene further.

Why not look at the **Content Browser** and see what else fits in the scene, other than barrels, for additional practice?

Progress in Urban Warrior, so far

Believe it or not, we have now acquired, after completing the preceding tasks, most of the fundamental skills needed to put together not just Urban Warrior but just about any type of a game with an environment!

Everything else we do in this book (and I suspect many of your future projects after that) hinges on understanding the preceding concepts, so it was important that we started with the bare basics.

For example, all of the buildings inside of our level are first going to be built using brushes, and while later we will replace some of them with static meshes, we will still use them in other areas as we try to optimize our game for the iOS platform.

Lighting, and in particular photorealistic lighting, remains one of the biggest challenges in computer graphics these days. It is so important that some companies have people whose entire job is creating lighting for levels. Working with the iOS platform makes our lighting capabilities much lower than our PC counterparts making us stick to Point Lights for most of our implementation. *Chapter 6, Bringing It All Together,* talks briefly on how lighting can be used in designing combat scenarios, as lighting can often make or break a level.

Finally, when we add enemies to our game Urban Warrior (or **bots** as they are called in Unreal) or, for that matter, any type of inanimate, non-interactive detail such as scene props, it will be pretty much in the same way that we added our objects in earlier by using the **Content Browser.**

Pop quiz

1. Where can the Content Browser be found?

    a. In the Edit menu under Browser Windows

    b. By typing in Content Browser in the command prompt

    c. By clicking on the Content Browser button on the toolbox

    d. Both a and c

2. How do we make a point light brighter?

    a. Rebuilding our lighting makes everything brighter

    b. Use the scaling widget

    c. Change the brightness property inside the light's object properties

    d. Both b & c

3. What setting should the widget be set to to squash an object, brush, or static mesh?

    a. Scaling

    b. Translation

    c. Non-uniform Scaling

    d. Rotation

Summary

Hopefully you've enjoyed this chapter and are now less intimidated by the rich functionality of UDK!

We have quite a long way to go before we see our game realized, but we are making steady progress nonetheless. So far in this chapter we have already covered the following:

◆ A basic overview of the interface aspects of UDK you need to know, with particular focus on the functions needed to create basic content for a beginner/intermediate game designer

◆ How geometrical operations work

◆ How to put a virtual room together using these aforementioned geometrical operations

◆ How to texture this newly-created world

◆ How to illuminate and light this world

◆ How to enrich it with 3D models other than basic geometry from UDK's repository

In the next chapter, we will delve deeper into using UDK and we'll start laying out the foundations for the game in more detail, looking at more advanced operations related and connected to the ones covered in this chapter. We'll also see what the specific implications/limitations of this are; how far can we start pushing the engine in its mobile capacity before we compromise important aspects of game play such as the frame rate?

3
Taking It to the Next Level: Enriching with Content

At this point, we have a textured room and some barrels around it. This is nice and all, but in order to give the suspension of disbelief that we want our players to have while playing the game, we need to add some other things to make our world believable.

In this chapter we shall:

◆ Put our current level on the grid and create an exterior area

◆ Create a custom sky dome that can be used on mobile devices

◆ Learn about lighting and how it is used on the iOS platform

◆ Use the Mobile Preview option to show how our level looks on an iOS device

◆ Add particles to breathe life into our world

◆ Use fog to hide objects in the distance for efficiencies

With that being said, let's begin!

The outside world

Game levels take place in a large variety of different places. Inside space stations, epic fantasy towns, a forest, even someone's own back yard. Something that all of these places have in common is that we use the same basic tools in order to make every kind of environment that we can imagine! You'll see how we can easily expand on what we've done here and afterwards in *Chapter 6*, *Bringing It All Together*, we will explore how Geometry mode can make blocking out an area really easy, but for now, let's create a door.

Time for action – creating an exterior

At the moment, we have a single room that is textured and has some objects in it. This is great, but we can take some steps to expand this world to create something even better! First though, let's regroup and make sure we are all on the same page.

1. From the top menu, select **View | Viewport Configuration | 2x1 Split**.

> There are many different options that you can use in determining how UDK is displayed and works for you, and I encourage you to take the time to figure out what you like and don't like. While having a **Front** viewport is fine, I like having a larger screen space for the **Perspective** view so I have a better idea of what the area I'm creating looks like. This is more my personal preference than anything, but it is what I will be using from now on.

2. From the **Top** viewport, hold *Ctrl + Alt* and drag from slightly higher on the top left-hand side to past the bottom right-hand side of the room that we've created.

While holding *Ctrl + Alt* and dragging the mouse you will notice a red rectangle being created. When you let go of the right mouse button all of the objects inside of the area will be selected. This is useful for selecting many objects at once inside an area.

If you cannot see the whole room inside the viewport, move back using the scroll wheel on the mouse. To move inside a viewport, you will first need to click inside it. To drag the screen, hold the right mouse button and drag in the direction you want to move it.

3. Zoom into the top left-hand side of the room and right-click on the top vertices on the left-hand side. You should notice the room snapping to the grid. If you do not see anything happen, you are either perfectly aligned or you have the grid lock off. To enable it again, there is a checkbox on the right-hand side of a number with half of a grid on the left-hand side. Make sure that that checkbox is checked. Right-click inside of the **Side** viewport and right-click on the top vertices on the left-hand side.

> At this point our room now fits to the grid. We want to build to the grid so that it will be easier for us to make sure that everything is seamless and we don't have holes inside of our geometry, which is a common problem that I see when people are starting out in UDK. Also note that right-clicking on a vertex moves the widget to that vertex. If you wanted to rotate an object by a certain vertex, this would be how you could do that.

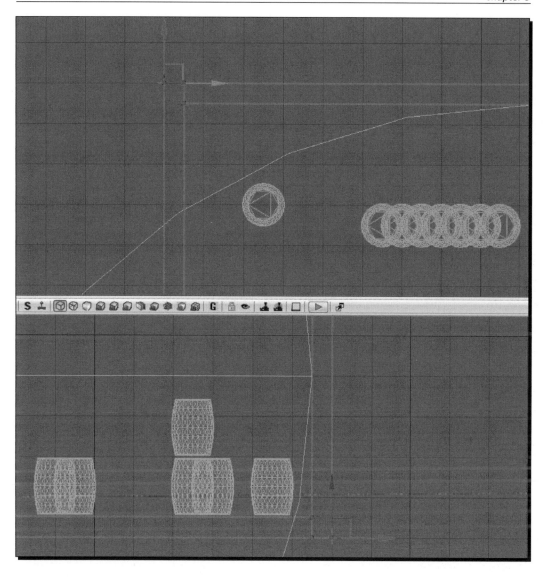

4. Save your level and click on **Build All**. When finished, you will notice that the level looks the same, though it may have shifted a bit.

5. Next confirm that the grid spacing size is **16**. If the number is lower than **16**, press the] key until it is **16**. If it is higher than **16**, press the [key. You should see the grid on the level change based on what keys were pressed.

6. Left-click on the brush on the left-hand side in the **Top** viewport. Right-click to enter the **Perspective** viewport and adjust your view so that you can see the middle of the wall.

Remember, you may hold the left-hand side button to look left and right, right to pan, and both to move forward or backward. To zoom in and out in the viewport, simply use the scroll wheel. Another option for moving is holding the right mouse button and using the *W, A, S,* and *D* keys to move around like you would in a first person shooter.

7. On the **Side** viewport, click on the button that looks like a 3D cube to go into **Geometry Mode**. Right-click on the top vertices on the left-hand side of the brush and make sure you are in translation mode by either clicking on the menu icon that looks like four arrows crossing or pressing the *Space bar* until you see the arrows for translation.

8. Hold the *Alt* key and drag the brush down using the red arrow in the **Top** viewport moving it down until you reach slightly less than half way through the brush.

    You should notice the object moving, but when you let go, you will see two brushes in its place. We have effectively made a copy of the previous wall for us to use to create a door.

9. Drag the **Top** viewport down to the bottom of our newly created brush by holding, right-clicking, and dragging up. Holding *Ctrl + Alt,* select both vertices at the bottom of the wall. You should see the two blue squares change to red. Drag those vertices up until they are close to the other end of the brush, with enough space existing to create a door.

10. Using *Ctrl + Alt* in **Geometry Mode** will only select the vertices of the selected objects, which can be useful for only altering small parts of a larger object without worrying about things.

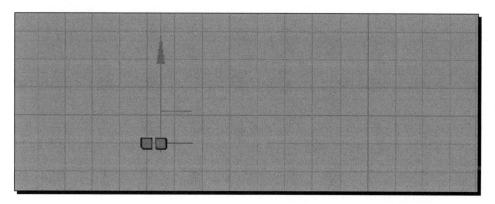

11. In the **Side** viewport hold *Ctrl + Alt* and select the bottom of our door and drag the object to be at the same level as the floor we created earlier. Next, select the last two vertices and drag it down so that it is higher than a person would go through, but with space for an overhead area for the door. I made mine 12 squares tall (at 16 units a box).

12. Switch back to **Camera Mode** (click on the **Camera** icon next to the **Geometry Mode** icon) and press *F4* to access the properties of the door brush. Under the **CSR Oper** option, select **CSG_Subtract**.

13. You should notice that the door changes its color to a golden color. Now if you were to use **Build Geometry,** you would see an opening in our wall. This is because what a **Subtractive** brush does is remove anything that would have been added to the level, hence the name **Subtractive**.

Note that you could also create a subtractive brush by using the **Builder Brush** and selecting the button to the left-hand side of the **CSG_Add** button in the **Brush** toolbar. Both are completely valid to use, but as we are building to the grid now, having shapes in the correct placement is critical.

14. In the **Perspective** viewport, left-click on the wall and select **Find in Content Browser**. You will notice that inside the content browser the material that we used before will be selected. Left-click on a side of the door. Afterwards, right-click on that same side and select **Select Surfaces | Matching Brush**. Notice that now all the sides of the door are highlighted. With that, right-click again and select **Apply Material :NEC_Walls_BSP_Brick1** to apply a material to it.

15. In the **Side** viewport, click on the floor. Right-click into the **Top** viewport to change viewports and then use the **Translate** tool to move the floor in front of the door.

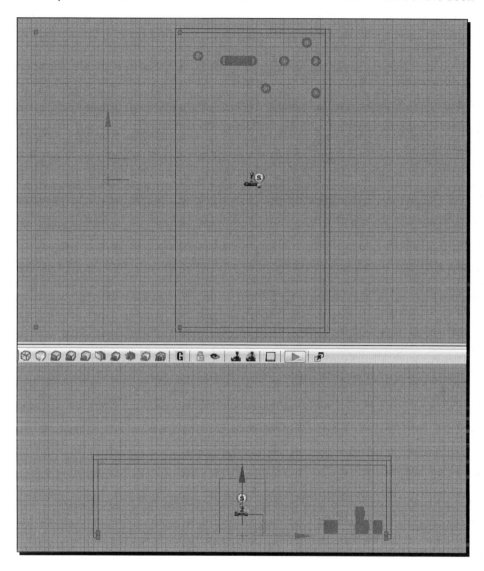

16. Rebuild the map and you should see some new ground outside of the door.

    You may notice that it takes a lot more time now in order to build the lighting. This is because now that the room is open, it is trying to draw the point lights influence inside the entire world. However, we only care about the room and the area immediately outside of the room which won't take nearly for a while. In UDK, we use something called a **Lightmass Importance Volume** to let the level know which areas are important and which are not.

17. Duplicate the floor again, but in a downward direction on the **Side** viewport. Go into **Geometry** mode and extend each of the sides of the box until the box is completely filling our two rooms. Right-click on the brush and select **Convert | Convert to Volume | Lightmass Importance Volume.** The color of the box should now be a yellowish color.

18. Save and rebuild the map. You should notice that it takes a lot less time now to build.

19. Press *Alt + 3* to go into **Unlit** mode to make it easier for us to see what we are doing. Go into the **Content Browser** and pick out material to use for the floor of our outside area, **Material'UN_Terrain.Dirt.M_UN_Terrain_Dirt_04'**, which is located in the **UN_Terrain** package. Once you have left-clicked on the material you want to use, right-click on a selected wall in the **Perspective** viewport and select **Add Material : M_UN_Terrain_Dirt_04**. You could also just type in **Dirt** in the search bar located in the **Content Browser**.

20. Back in the content browser, you'll find our building's exterior **NEC_Walls.BSP. Materials.M_NEC_Walls_BSP_Ceramic2**, which you can find inside **NEC_Walls** or if you type in **Walls** into the **Content Browser**, it will show up.

21. Once the material has been added, open up the service properties by going to **View | Surface Properties**. Click on the drop box under **Simple** and select **2.0** then click on the **Apply** button. You should notice the material matching the building perfectly.

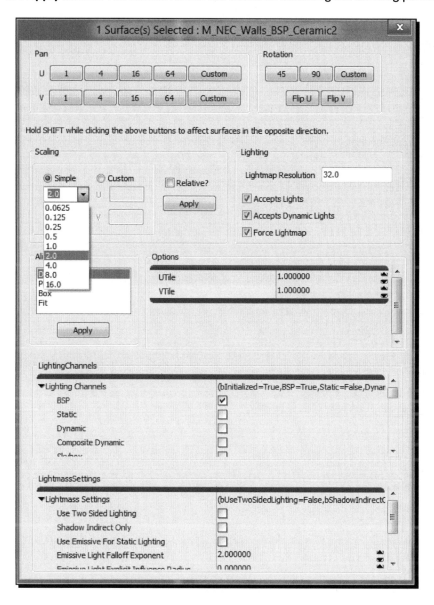

22. Go into the **Content Browser** select to find **Static Meshes** in the **Object Type** section and type in **Sky** to find a skydome for us to use **StaticMesh'UN_Sky.SM.Mesh.S_UN_Sky_SM_SkyDome03'**. Right-click on the floor you created and select **Add Static Mesh : S_UN_Sky_SM_SkyDome03'**.

23. With the skydome selected, move it, so that the room we created is the center of the object. Rotate the skydome 180 degrees in order to have the sun face our door.

Skydomes are supposed to be quite large in order to create the illusion that it is the sky; if it was too small we would notice the sky moving along with us, which at the speed we're moving, would seem quite illogical.

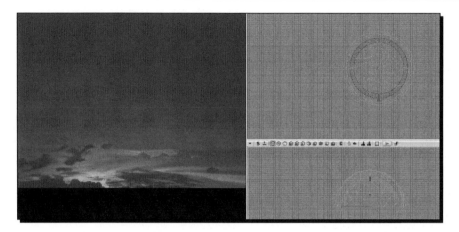

24. Press *F4* with the skydome selected, to go to its properties. Within the **Static Mesh Actor** section, go to the **Static Mesh Component**, and go to **Lighting** and turn **Accept Lights** and **Cast Shadows** off by clicking on the checkbox. Inside **Collision,** set the **Collision Type** to **COLLIDE_NoCollision**. Now that we have the sky, let's add some light to the world. Press *Alt + 4* to go back into **Lit** mode.

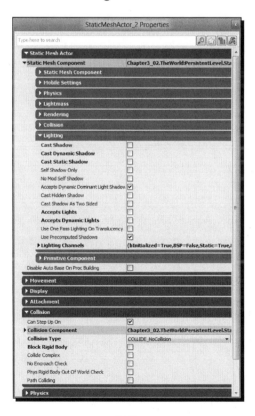

Next, go into the **Content Browser** and find the texture being used for the skybox which is **Material'UN_Sky.SM.Materials.M_UN_Sky_SM_Sunset01'**. Right-click on it, and select **Create a Copy**. From the menu that pops up, change the **Package** name to something unique such as `Chapter3` then click on **OK**.

25. The new page that has been brought up is your new package. Double-click on the new material that you added to enter the **Material Editor**. In the **Material Editor** go to the **Properties** window on the bottom until you find the **Mobile Allow Fog** property and uncheck it.

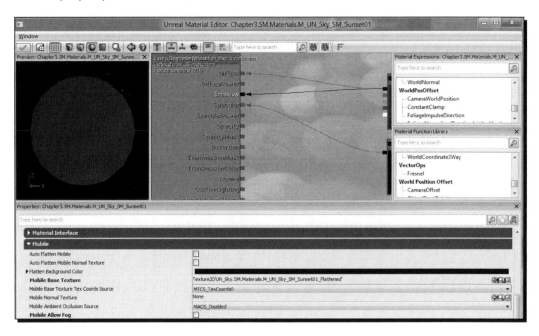

26. Log out of the **Material Editor** (Saying **Yes** to saving the material). Right-click on the new package you created and save it to the directory that contains your map.

27. Go into the skydome's object properties one more time by pressing *F4*. In the **Search** box, type in **Material** and hit the + symbol on the first section you see. With the new material we created selected inside the **Content Browser**, click on the little green arrow pointing to the left-hand side.

28. We are replacing the previous skybox material with one of our own. Sadly, the Unreal default doesn't account for mobile users, so if a level is created without that checkmark done, it will look like a large single colored screen.

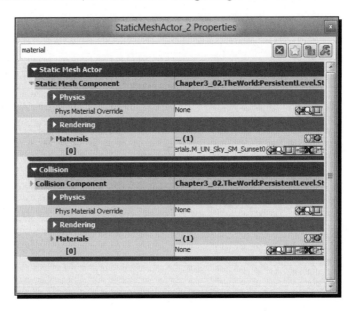

29. Go into the **Actor Classes** panel by selecting **View | Browser Windows | Actor Classes**. From there, left-click on the **Directional Light** actor located in **Lights | DirectionalLights | DirectionalLight**.

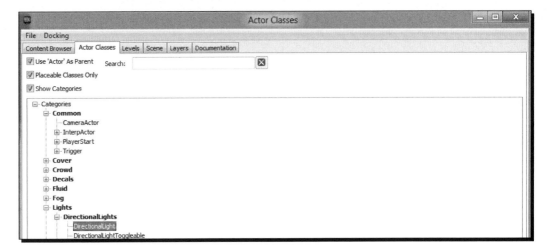

30. Those of you who are familiar with UDK may want to use a **Dominant Directional Light**, but unlike the PC, iOS does not have support for it, so in order to use a directional light, use the simple **DirectionalLight** class.

31. With the **DirectionalLight** selected, press *Space bar* until you reach the rotation tool, which means that the tool changes to look like circles. Rotate the **Directional Light** you created so that the arrow connected to it faces the direction the sun in your level is pointed at.

32. With that finished, press *F4* to enter the **Object Properties** menu. Select the **Light Color** property inside the **Light Component** of the object and set the color to something to reflect the area. I used the dropper tool and selected a lighter color that will make the area look like a sunrise/sunset.

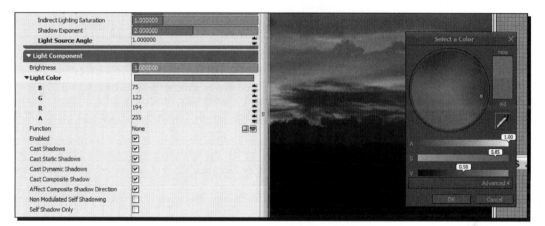

33. Set the **Brightness** to 1.4.

With **Brightness** it is important to not have the value too high and I recommend not going above 2.5. With a PC, it is perfectly possible to go higher than 2.5, but due to limitations of the iOS device, it is possible for greenings to occur which means that if a light is too bright, it looks greener due to the fact that there is more memory available in the green channel of colors.

34. Create a duplicate of the light that you created and rotate it in the opposite direction that you created the current light. Change the **Brightness** of the light to 0.25 and change the color to the opposite of the color you used before. To do this, open up the color wheel. You will see the location of your current color on the wheel displayed. In the opposite X and Y direction, you will find what is known as the color's opposite. In general, red's opposite is green and blue's opposite is yellow. This is shown in the following screenshot:

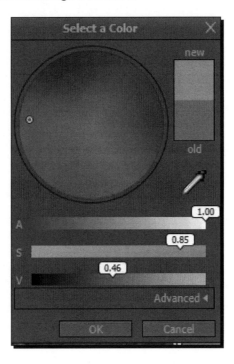

35. Build our game by selecting **Build | Build All** and clicking on **Close** when finished.

36. Save your project and start your game by clicking on the **Start Mobile Previewer** button on the main toolbar saying **Yes** when it asks you to save the package. It looks as shown in the following screenshot:

What just happened?

We now have our first outdoor environment in the Unreal Engine and have built some fundamental knowledge that will serve us well when we start production on our game Urban Warrior!

Previewing the mobile editor

There is a button in the top bar that looks like a small phone with a brown screen that, when highlighted, says **Emulate Mobile Features**. When clicked, this will change your display to look closer to what it will look like on the iOS device, and is a better tool to use while doing lighting. In my experience, Unreal tends to make things either too dark or too light, so it can be a challenge to find something that works well on both an iOS device and PC. If you are trying to create a game for both systems, you may want to have two separate forms of lighting and test it on the actual device until you are happy with it.

Particles make everything better

The world we live in is very complex and certain things, such as explosions and fires, are very hard to replicate inside a game engine, due to a number of factors, but mostly due to the limitations of what is possible to do at 60/30 frames per second (fps). The best way to do this at a small cost is to use something called a **particle system**. Some of the many things you can do include creating smoke, electric sparks, falling leaves, snow, dust, and fantasy elements like magic spells. Particles are usually subtle in games, but it is often the little things that make the biggest impact on us in creating the suspension of disbelief that we are going for in our games.

 It is worth noting that while particles are a relatively easy way to add special effects on a mobile device, they can also be one of the more expensive things to add to your level. This can be due to a number of factors; alpha blending caused by sprite-based particle systems heavily taxes the GPU's fill rate, while particle systems with high particle counts heavily tax the CPU due to an increased count of objects to update every frame. There's a fine balance to be found on mobile in this regard, and the right balance will heavily depend on what else is going on in the game. Playtesting your game on your intended device is the best way to see just how much your game can handle things. For more information on optimizations and debugging your games, see *Chapter 7, Advanced Content Creation for Urban Warrior*.

Time for action – adding a particle system

For starters, let's place an emitter to our level of leaves falling from a tree. That being said, let's add a tree to our level too.

1. Open the **Content Browser** and find **StaticMesh'GenericFoliage01.Trees.Mesh.SM_ GEN_Foliage01_LargeTree01_Opt'**. Left-click on it and exit the **Content Browser**. Right-click on the floor and select **Add Actor | Load StaticMesh'GenericFoliage01. Trees.Mesh.SM_GEN_Foliage01_LargeTree01_Opt'**. After it loads in the tree, right-click on the floor and select **Add StaticMesh: GenericFoliage01.Trees.Mesh. SM_GEN_Foliage01_LargeTree01_Opt'**.

2. With the tree selected, press the *Space bar* until you get to the **Scaling Mode** (the widget's arrows are replaced by large red boxes). Click-and-drag down until the tree is shrunk to a manageable size.

3. Back in the Content Browser, toggle **Particle Systems** in the **Object Type** and you should see **ParticleSystem'Envy_Level_Effects_2.CTF_Crisis_Energy.Falling_Leaf'**.

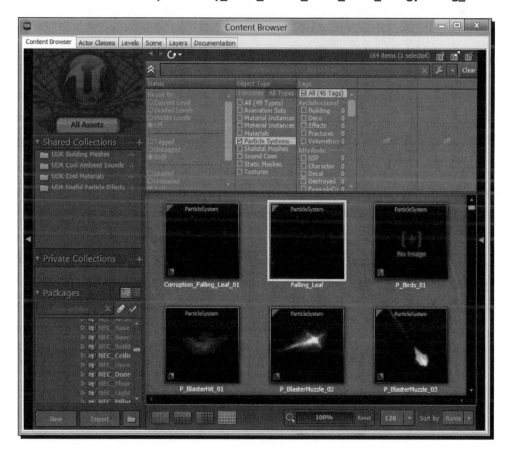

4. With the object selected, go back into the **Perspective** viewport and right-click on the floor, load the particle system, and then add it to the level. This will create an icon that looks like five circles of different colors.

5. It will be too large, so you will need to scale it down as discussed previously. I moved the emitter to the middle of the tree for leaves to fall from it.

6. Build our game by selecting **Build | Build All** and clicking on **Close** when finished.

7. Save your project and start your game by clicking on the **Start Mobile Previewer** button on the main toolbar, saying **Yes** when it asks you to save the package. You will see the resulting screen as shown in the following screenshot:

What just happened?

With a few simple steps, we have now added a simple particle system into our level's world. Taking time after creating our game, adding little features like this will do a lot to help the game become more and more immersive. You may have noticed right now that the leaves have a black background to them. We will be fixing that when we talk about importing textures of our own in the next chapter.

Foggy weather

One of the primary things about working on a mobile device is that it is going to be impossible to render a large sprawling world with large landscapes without some neat tricks. One of the ways that the Unreal Engine makes it possible for us to have large levels is the ability to create fog.

Like most things that you will run into on mobile devices, this is quite a balancing act. Fog on mobile devices should really only be considered in extreme cases where large view distances would cause significant visual pop in, or where the fog distance is low enough that a significant amount of the level will be culled. Testing is really the only thing that can be used here to determine if it's worth it.

Time for action – adding fog

Adding fog is incredibly easy to do for mobiles; however, note that you will not be able to see this fog in the PC version as it uses its own system for implementing it.

1. Duplicate the tree we created in the previous section and move it some distance away from our other one.

   We will be using this tree as a test of what objects that are far away will look like when we enable fog in our game.

2. Open up the **World Properties** menu by selecting **View | World Properties**.

3. In the **Mobile** section, check the **Fog Enabled** option.

4. Set the **Fog Color** to be something that will blend in with our skybox. The following screenshot shows the values that I used:

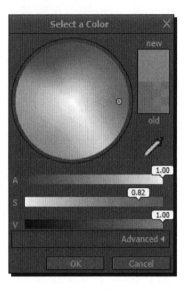

5. Change the **Fog Start** to a high number so that you don't see things fade away so quickly.

 Note that it's possible to set **Use Gamma Correction** which, when set, will attempt to make the lighting fit to be more like it is on the PC, but it has a performance cost. You'll have to evaluate if you think it is worth using it in your titles.

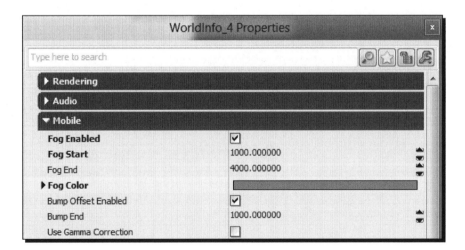

6. Build our game by selecting **Build | Build All** and clicking on **Close** when finished.

7. Save your project and start your game by clicking on the **Start Mobile Previewer** button on the main toolbar, saying **Yes** when it asks you to save the package. You will see the screen as shown in the following screenshot:

What just happened?

We've now added fog to our game, adding to the efficiency that we will be experiencing at runtime as well as adding? a tool that can be used to create atmosphere in your game. Play around with the values to get a feel for what the changes mean and see what feels the most comfortable to use.

Summary

We have now learned a lot of aspects that will come in handy when creating our game Urban Warrior. We've specifically learned:

- How to put our current level on the grid and create an exterior area
- How skydomes are used on mobile devices
- Lighting and how it is used on the iOS platform
- How to use the Mobile Preview option to show how our level looks on an iOS device
- How particles can breathe life into our world
- How to use fog to hide objects in the distance for efficiencies

Now that we have this firm basis to build upon in building levels, we will now learn about the Unreal Engine's built-in visual scripting language Kismet and how it can help us do even more amazing things to our levels!

4
Using Kismet and Matinee

In the previous chapters, we have learned how the basic interface of UDK works and how to build a basic environment. This is all well and good, but at the moment, all we can do is walk in the world while looking around. Don't we wish we could do something there?

*In this chapter, we are going to take a look at **Kismet** and **Matinee**, two of the most popular ways to create motion in our otherwise static world. This should help breathe life into the world of our game. After all, actions do speak louder than words.*

In this chapter we shall:

◆ Learn what Kismet is and what we can do with it

◆ Use Kismet to change our project's viewpoint to a third-person perspective

◆ Discuss Kismet and the benefits and drawbacks of its usage

◆ Learn about the Matinee editor

◆ Create a cinematic using Matinee

◆ Use both Kismet and Matinee to create an automatic door

◆ Learn about sequence objects specifically made for mobile devices

◆ Learn about Mobile Input and add functionality to our iOS game

But before we dive into creating new things for our game, first let's get an understanding for what Kismet actually is and what it can be used for.

Defining Kismet

Kismet is a system of visual scripting in UDK that makes it possible for people to affect the game world and design gameplay events. For teams without a programmer, Kismet can be a Godsend; it makes it possible for someone without any coding knowledge to do things that would otherwise require the use of **UnrealScript**, a programming language that the Unreal Engine uses.

In order to create a sequence of events, you have to connect a series of sequence objects together. This, in turn, generates code when the game is run, which causes it to do the things that you said it should do. It would be easy for me to write a book entirely about things that can be done in Kismet, but as we are planning on creating a third person shooter for the iOS, I will refrain from straying too far from that. However, we will be discussing the creation of more and more complex sequences as the book progresses.

Creating your first Kismet sequence

Now that we've learned what Kismet is and what it can do for us, let's see it used in action and see how easy it is to get results!

Time for action – changing the level to a third-person perspective

The default perspective given to players in UDK is first-person. Let's say we want it to be in third-person instead. It will be quite easy to do so due to Epic's console command which does just that. However, in order to first simplify learning Kismet as much as possible and practice what we've learned in previous chapters, we are going to be starting from scratch with a new level.

1. First, create a new map by selecting **File | New...** and then choose one of the four options at the top. I personally chose **Midday Lighting**.

Bring up the **World Properties** menu by selecting **View | World Properties** from the menu bar at the top of the UDK interface. Type Game Type in the **Search** bar at the top of the **World Properties** menu, which will bring up the **Game Type** menu and the options relevant to us. From there, change the drop-down menus on both **Default Game Type** and **Game Type for PIE** to **UTDeathmatch**. While we are there in the **Zone Info** section, under **KillZ**, set the value to -1000.

2. Now, before we get into Kismet, I want to explain what it is exactly that we are doing. Start up your game using the **Play | InEditor** option. This starts up your game as it would be seen on the PC, so it is not representative of how the project will look on an iOS device, but it will be easier to demonstrate the following change. When the game appears, press the *Tab* key and you will see a black bar appear on the screen. This is the console window, which can be used to execute different commands that Unreal has built in. The one we are going to be using right now, will toggle first and third person modes. With the console open, type in behindview 1 and press *Enter*:

You can also press the tilde (~) key to access the console window which will show all things logged during play as well as commands you've previously entered.

3. As you can see, the game switches your character to a third person mode. One of the cool things about Kismet is we can, in fact, call these commands for the player, which is what we'll be doing in this demonstration.

4. Open up the Kismet interface by clicking on the **K** icon at the top of the UDK interface on the main toolbar. You should see a new window pop up that may look a bit daunting, but it's not too bad once you know what everything is.

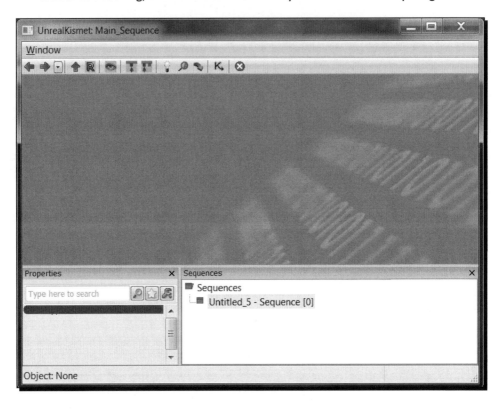

5. Underneath the menu bars, you will see a large area with a lot of 1s and 0s on it. This is our workspace and where we will be placing all of the Sequence Objects that we create.

6. The bottom two bars are the **Properties** and **Sequences** windows. The **Properties** window will hold all of the data that we will want to set within the sequence objects, that we will be creating which can be accessed when we left-click on them. All of our work in this chapter will be in the same sequence, so we will not need to use the **Sequences** window, but we will be going over it in *Chapter 5, Action Sequences for Urban Warrior*.

7. Right-click anywhere inside the large area in the upper portion of the interface. Choose to create a **Player Spawned** event by choosing **New Event** | **Player** | **Player Spawned** from the menu that pops up.

8. Left-click on the **Player Spawned Event Sequence** object so that the **Properties** window comes up and change the value of **Max Trigger Count** from 1 to 0.

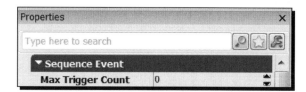

Having a value of 0 means that it can be triggered an infinite number of times.

9. Right-click under the instigator connection (the purple/pink arrow) and select **Create New Object Variable**.

10. Right-click and create a **Console Command** action by choosing **New Action | Misc | Console Command** from the menus.

11. Inside the properties, type `behindview 1` as the value for **Commands[0]**.

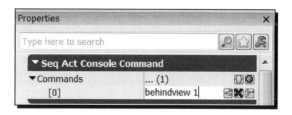

12. Connect the output from the **Player Spawned** event to the input of the **Console Command** action by clicking on the square on the right-hand side of the **Out** text on the **Player Spawned** event and dragging your mouse, until it reaches the black square on the left-hand side of the **In** text.

13. Connect the connector of both the **Instigator** and **Target** to the **Object** variable we created earlier.

By this point your Kismet should look similar to the following screenshot:

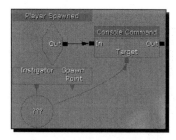

14. Now start your game by clicking on the **Start Mobile Previewer** button on the main toolbar. You will see the following screenshot:

What just happened?

Upon starting the game, when the player is spawned (the **Player Spawned** event is activated), we change our perspective to be in the third person (the **Console Command** action is called). We've also learned some fundamentals in working with Kismet and have an understanding of how sequence objects connect to create different effects. Not too shabby for only using two sequence objects.

Kismet primer

While working with Kismet, some of the terms may be difficult to understand at first, so I would like to quickly go over some aspects of Kismet in general.

Parts of a sequence object

Every node we work with is called a **sequence object,** because it is an object within a sequence. We will be talking more about sequences in *Chapter 6, Bringing It All Together*, but for now let's talk about the parts that make up a Kismet node.

The left-hand side of a sequence object is called the **Input**; while the right-hand side is called the **Output**. The following are the variables that are either values given to us, or that we set depending on the object.

There are four different kinds of sequence objects, three of which we will be using in this chapter and we will be using the fourth in *Chapter 5, Action sequences For Urban Warrior*. The following screenshot shows the sequence objects:

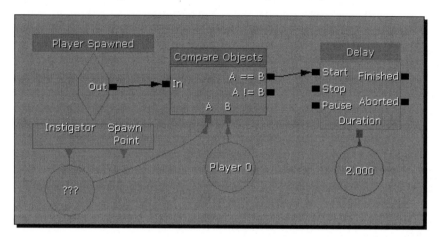

- ◆ **Events**: This is what all other sequence objects get called from. Code in Kismet only gets called if a certain thing happens, like the **Player Spawned** event that was called when the player spawns in our level. These objects are red and are shaped like diamonds.

- ◆ **Actions**: These perform a defined task when an event is triggered. This is the most used item, so it is the object with the most variety. The **Console Command** action, as well as the **Delay** used previously, is an example of an action. Actions are presented as rectangles.

- ◆ **Variables**: These are what hold information within our level. If another sequence object has squares underneath it, that is a spot that holds a variable. They are colored differently depending on what the variable actually is. The instigator in the **Player Spawned** event is a variable that is filled with our player's information when it is called, and the **Blue** number under the **Delay** variable in the previous screenshot is a float variable with the value of 2.0. We will be using variables extensively in *Chapter 6, Bringing It All Together*. Variables are represented as circles.

- ◆ **Conditions**: These actions are special in the fact that they can do different things based on the values of different objects used for comparing numbers or objects. They are used to control the flow of things within a sequence. The **Compare Objects** condition is an example of a condition. Conditions are traditionally blue and are rectangular.

Benefits and drawbacks of using Kismet

As with any job, it is important to use the tool that is appropriate for it. UDK provides three ways of giving interactivity to the game world: Kismet (which we are discussing), Matinee (which we are going to discuss), and UnrealScript (which is out of the scope of this book, but it is covered extremely well in *Unreal Development Kit Game Programming with UnrealScript: Beginner's Guide* by *Rachel Cordone* which is also available from Packt Publishing). All three have specific advantages and disadvantages to them, but Kismet is the one that I use most often.

As you expand your research into UDK after reading this book, you may see forum posts with people asking how to do something in Kismet. A lot of people will reply to telling them to learn UnrealScript instead. While they may seem arrogant, there are some reasons why they are saying to use that tool. I've included a list of pros and cons of Kismet which may help you, afterwards, in deciding if it is the correct tool for what you're working on.

Benefits of using Kismet

Kismet is a wonderful tool and is a great starting point when first starting out with UDK. Some other benefits associated with Kismet are:

- **Having a lower barrier to entry**: No programming knowledge is needed so it is easier to get started and you can start creating games now.

- **Great for prototyping gameplay mechanics**: Saying a mechanic is going to be fun is one thing, but no one is going to believe you unless you can prove it. Kismet makes it extremely easy to get something up quickly. As a designer, having something to show a programmer will make it much easier for them to translate to code.

- **Great for one-off events**: If your level needs to have something specific or only at a specific time or level events like an explosion, Kismet is a great tool to use.

- **Easier to see the flow of events**: If you are more of a visual thinker or like to stare at something to see the big picture, it is a lot easier to use Kismet. The Sequence Objects and colors all mean something specific to make it easy to discern what is going on within a specific scene.

- **Easily extendable with UnrealScript**: With knowledge of how UnrealScript works, it is possible to create custom sequence objects of your own to create actions of your very own. If your game would have a dialogue system, creating a custom **Show Dialog** action would be possible in Kismet to make it easy to create entire dialog trees within Kismet.

Drawbacks

However, Kismet is not the be-all and end-all solution for everything that can possibly be done with UDK. Here are some of the drawbacks that using Kismet may have:

◆ **Complexity issues**: As you get more comfortable using Kismet, you will probably try to do more and more complex things with it (I know I have). If you are not careful you may have problems reading what your code is actually doing. Basically, the more complex a sequence gets, the harder it is to read.

◆ **Reiterations**: Many times in a game, you will want to have the same thing happen if you interact with a similar or identical object, like a door. If you want the same behavior with multiple objects or multiple levels, you have to paste it every single time you want to have that action happen. This can quickly stockpile into a really large amount of sequence objects which could be avoided if you wrote an UnrealScript file with the same behavior and made that object use that file to execute the actions within it.

◆ **Level Specific**: In much the same way Kismet is also specific to just the level that it is created in. For instance, if we wanted to create ten levels in our game, we would have to do the console command event in every single level. With UnrealScript, this would be built into the code base for the game and be automatic for all levels of the game.

◆ **Kismet can't do everything you'd like to in a game**: The truth is that the game Unreal Engine 3 was created to make a **First Person Shooter** (**FPS**), and the further you stray from that path, the harder it is going to be to create your game. That's not to say UDK can't be used to create other games. It's just going to be much more difficult as the sequence objects in Kismet are meant to create an FPS.

◆ **More custom behavior requires UnrealScript**: Continuing with the previous point, most of the time a game does something such as a game mechanics that UDK doesn't seem to do (like the Scarecrow boss battles in *Batman: Arkham Asylum*, "Plasmids" in *Bioshock 1* and *2,* or the jet packs in *Dark Void*). These examples probably use UnrealScript or C++ code to achieve the desired result.

◆ **Kismet is slower than UnrealScript**: While it will not matter with the project that we are creating now, as Kismet is basically a prewritten UnrealScript executed in a certain order, Kismet is slower than what could be achieved using just UnrealScript, and something that your game will continuously use would best be done with UnrealScript.

Have a go hero – Kismet

Console commands can do a lot of different things, giving you access to a lot of prewritten code including opening other maps (open levelname), and quitting the game (quit).

Try to make the game open another map when you start the level.

Defining Matinee

The **Matinee** tool is the driving force of all cinematic effects within the Unreal Engine. It gives users the ability to be the director within your game, giving you control over the camera, actor's movement, sound, as well as different cuts and animation effects. Think of any moment in an Unreal game where you didn't have direct control over the character, like a cutscene. Chances are, that was done in Matinee. However, Matinee can be used for many other things which we will discuss later.

In order to create a Matinee, we will use the (aptly named) Matinee Editor which can be accessed from within the Kismet menu.

Creating your first Matinee movie

Having defined what Matinee is used for, let's begin using it.

Time for action – opening cutscene

As things are, when the game begins we are brought straight into the action with no prior warning. In order to prepare the player and give them an idea of where they are, let's create a cutscene!

1. Go to the **Actor Classes** browser **View | Browser Windows | Actor Classes**. From there, you will see a list of classes that we can place within our level. Left-click on the **CameraActor** selection.

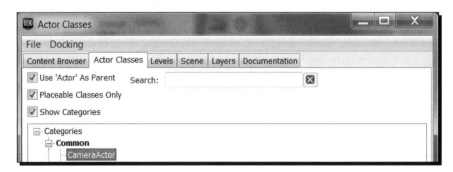

2. Close out the **Actor Classes** browser and right-click anywhere in your level. From the menu that pops up, select **Create CameraActor Here**. This will create an actor on the ground, in the spot in the spot where you clicked. It may be a good idea to position the camera above the player and looking at it.

3. If it isn't already up, open the Kismet editor by clicking on the **K** icon at the top of the UDK interface on the main toolbar.

4. Create a new Matinee by right-clicking inside the large area in the upper portion of the interface and selecting **New Matinee**. You should see an orange square pop out with a lot of different inputs and outputs.

5. Double-click on the object to enter the Matinee editor as shown in the following screenshot:

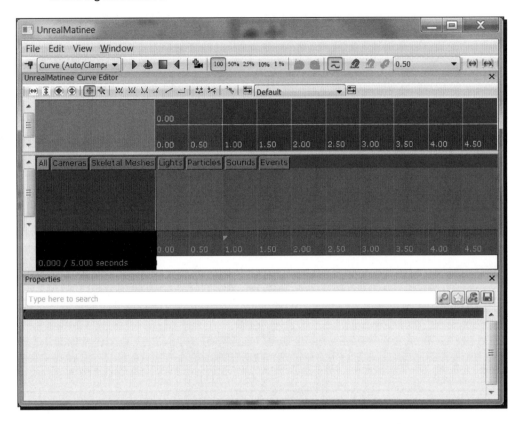

6. Minimize Matinee and select your **CameraActor** on the main screen by left-clicking on it and then bringing Matinee up. Right-click inside the **Group List** (the dark-grey column below all the tabs with text and at left-hand side to the timeline.) From the **Context** menu that appears, click on **Add New Camera Group**. When prompted for a name type in Camera.

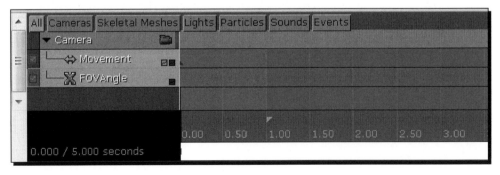

7. If you click on the little camera icon in the top-left of the **Camera** group, you will see the **Perspective** viewport changes into the camera's view.

8. If the camera icon doesn't show up, that means the camera is not connected to the group. To fix this, left-click on your camera inside the editor and then go back into Kismet. From there, right-click below the **Camera** text in the Matinee that we have created and select **Create New Object Var Using CameraActor_0** and connect it to the **Camera** slot.

9. Click on the **Movement** track on the **Camera** and then click on the first keyframe (the red triangle located in the timeline). You will notice that the bottom of the **Perspective** viewport changes its text to **ADJUST KEY Movement0**. Now if you move within the viewport, it will transfer over to the Camera actor that we have created. Once you have moved your camera to the spot where you want it, click outside of the keyframe in the Matinee window.

10. Right-click underneath **Camera** and select **Add New Director Group**.

11. Left-click on the **Director** track and then click on the **Add Key** icon which is the first icon just below the **File** menu (circled in the following screenshot in red) to add a new keyframe,to say, we want to use a different camera at this position. Select to use **Camera for the Cut To Group** and click on **OK**.

12. Left-click on the **Movement** track again. Drag the time slider from **0.00** to the **2.00** second mark, to the grey bar along the bottom of the Matinee area where all of the numbers are located.

13. Left-click on the **Add Key** icon to add a new keyframe to our movie. If all goes well, you should see something similar to the following screenshot:

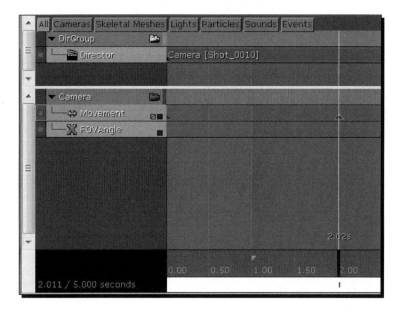

14. With the keyframe selected, move the camera closer to the player. At this point, if you drag the time slider, you will notice that the camera moves between the two points that we have created over the course of two seconds.

15. Left-click somewhere else on the timeline to remove the focus on the keyframe. Move the mouse scroller down in order to zoom-out from the timeline. You will notice a pink triangle pointing outwards at the 5.00 mark. That object marks the ending of the Matinee sequence, so click on it and drag it to the second mark.

16. You can also right-click on it and select **Move to Longest Track Endpoint** and it will automatically snap to the last keyframe added.

17. Close up Matinee and bring Kismet back up. Right-click next to the **Console Command** action that we created earlier, and select **NewAction | Toggle | ToggleCinematicMode**.

18. Inside the properties for the **ToggleCinematicMode**, disable the **HidePlayer** option. Connect the **Target** to the **Instigator** from the **Player Spawned** event we created in the previous example. Left-click on the sequence object and copy it by pressing *Ctrl + C*.

19. Paste the sequence object by pressing *Ctrl + V* and move the created sequence object to the right-hand side of the Matinee by holding *Ctrl* and dragging while it is selected.

20. Remove the connections to the **Console Command** action by holding the *Alt* key and clicking on the **In** and **Out** connectors. Drag the action next to the second **Toggle Cinematic Mode** action by clicking on it, holding *Ctrl* and dragging it over. Connect the **Out** from the **Player Spawned** action to the **Enable** of the first **Toggle Cinematic Mode**. Connect that **Out** to the **Play** of the Matinee, connect the **Completed** output to the **Disable** input of the second Toggle Cinematic Mode, and finally, connect the **Out** on the **Toggle Cinematic Mode** to the input on the **Console Command**.

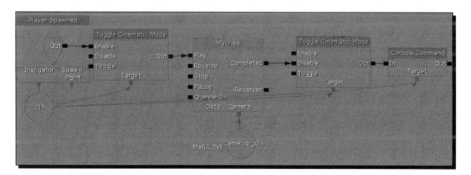

21. Save your project (**File | Save**) and start your game by clicking on the **Start Mobile Previewer** button on the main toolbar.

What just happened?

We have created our first cinematic moment in Unreal! Now when our game starts, we zoom into our character enabling our players to get ready for the action leading up ahead. While it may have been a bit of a hassle to get such a simple movement, it is easy to see the great potential to create many exciting things with the Matinee tool!

Have a go hero – Matinee

You can easily add more key points to this opening cutscene and extend its length to as long as you want. You can also add another **CameraActor** and switch between cameras while the movie is going on. Take some time to coast through your level and maybe spin around the player as the game begins.

With our powers combined...

Now that we have learned some fundamentals of using Kismet and Matinee, let's do a non-trivial example of something that can be done with them both together.

Time for action – creating an automatic door

If your game takes place somewhere that humans reside, chances are you are going to have a door, and as a player, we are drawn to them to continue a level. With that in mind, let's create a door that will automatically open for us when someone comes near it, and close when it is empty.

1. Go back into the main editor window and access the **Content Browser** via **View | BrowserWindows | ContentBrowser**.

2. In the **Object Type** tab, check the **Static Meshes** option as we only want to see Static Meshes. In the top search bar, type in `doorway`. Left-click on the mesh selected and close the **Content Browser**.

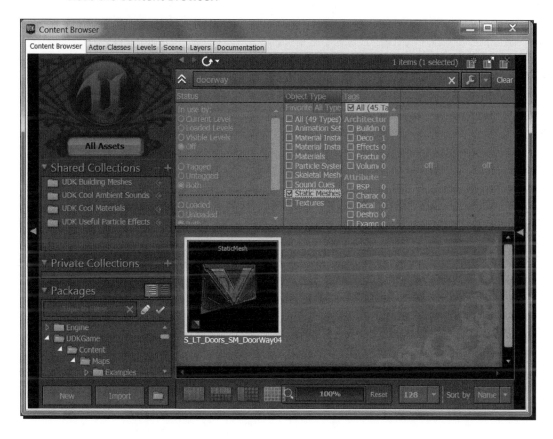

3. Right-click somewhere in your level and select **AddActor | LoadStaticMesh:S_LT_ Doors_SM_DoorWar04**. Right-click again and select **Add Static StaticMesh:S_LT_ Doors_SM_DoorWar04**.

4. Right-click on the door we placed and select **Convert |
ConvertStaticMeshActortoMover**.

5. Go into the properties for the door (*F4*) and type `collision` into the search bar. Change the **CollisionType** variable on the bottom to **COLLIDE_BlockAll**.

6. Use the **Builder Brush** and **Additive Geometry** discussed in *Chapter 2, Beginning Urban Warrior; a First Person Shooter* to build a brush on each side of the door and one on top that covers the entire distance above the door.

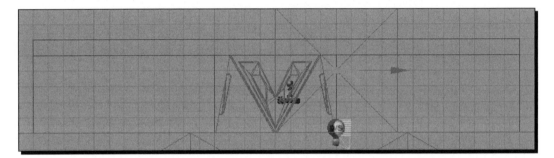

Notice how the brush does not go all the way to the door and, if we make the brush larger, it will cover part of the door. Luckily for us, there is an easy way to make the walls flush with the door we want to use.

7. Use the **Side** viewport and click on the button that looks like a 3D cube to go into **Geometry Mode**. Click on the right side brush and make sure you are in translation mode by either clicking on the menu icon that looks like four arrows crossing, or by pressing *Space*bar until you see the arrows to translate. Click on the top square at left-hand side to turn it red so that it is selected and drag it over to the edge of the door Do the opposite for the other brush.

I will be going over **Geometry Mode** and how it can be used to create gameplay areas and allow for fast prototyping of gameplay areas in *Chapter 6, Bringing It All Together*.

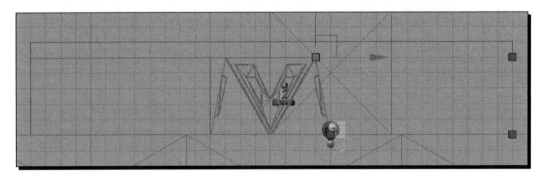

8. Use the **Top** viewport and create a brush that is in the middle of the door with space in front and behind the door. Right-click on that brush and select **Convert | ConverttoVolume | Trigger Volume** to change the brush into a trigger volume. After this, save your map and click on **Build All**.

9. Click on the **Trigger Volume** that we've created to select it and open the Kismet editor by clicking on the **K** icon at the top of the UDK interface on the main toolbar.

10. Right-click anywhere inside the large area in the upper portion of the interface. Create a **Trigger Volume Touch** event by choosing **New Event using TriggerVolume_0 | Touch** from the menu that pops up.

11. Left-click on the **TriggerVolume_0 Touch** event object so that the properties window comes up and change the value of **MaxTriggerCount** from 1 to 0.

12. We want to have a sound play when the door opens and when it closes, so create two **Play Sound** actions using **NewAction | Sound | PlaySound**.

13. Go into the **Content Browser** and change the object type you're looking for to **SoundCue** and change the search to just **door**. Select the first SoundCue **A_Door_Metal03_CloseStartCue** and go back into Kismet.

14. Select the bottom **Play Sound** action. Inside the properties, you should see an icon that looks like a green arrow pointing at the left-hand side, next to the **PlaySound** property. Click on that button and it should fill the box with the value of what you have selected in the **Content Browser**.

15. Repeat steps from step 13 to step 14 using **A_Door_Metal03_OpenStartCue** and the top **PlaySound** respectively.

16. Back in the editor, click on the door and go back into Kismet. Create a new Matinee object by right-clicking next to the **Touch Event** and selecting **NewMatinee**.

17. Go into the Matinee editor by double-clicking on the Matinee. Right-click inside the **Group List** and click on **AddNewCameraGroup**. When prompted for a name, type in Door.

18. Create a keyframe at the 0.50 position and, with it selected, left-click on the door in the **Perspective** viewport. Move the door to the left-hand side till it completely leaves the opening, making it possible for people to pass through.

19. Right-click on the end of the Matinee sequence (the pink triangle pointing out) and select **MovetoLongestTrackEndpoint**. Close Matinee and bring Kismet back up.

20. Connect the **Target** of both **Play Sound** actions to be the door in our Matinee sequence, so that we will hear the sound coming from the door.

21. From the **TriggerVolume_0 Touch** event connect the **Touched** output to the **Play** input on the top **Play Sound** event. Then, connect the **Empty** output to the **Play** input on the bottom **Play Sound** event. Connect the **Out** on the top **Play Sound** to the **Play** on the Matinee sequence. Connect the **Out** on the bottom **Play Sound** to the **Reverse** input on the Matinee sequence.

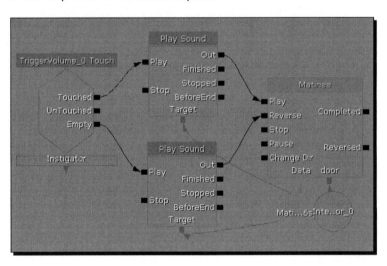

22. Save your project (**File | Save**) and start your game by clicking on the **Start Mobile Previewer** button on the main toolbar.

What just happened?

We have created one of the most used interactive objects within games: a door. With this basic idea, it is possible to do many similar things, such as moving platforms and elevators, as well as complex things like machinima using a game engine to create a cinematic production like *Rooster Teeth's Red versus Blue* or Epic's own *Samaritan* demo. There's plenty more you can do with Matinee, but it is best for you to explore on your own to discover things through experimentation.

Kismet for mobile devices

All of the examples we have seen can be and are used in the normal version of UDK and transfer to our mobile iOS game nicely. Most things in Kismet will work on mobiles as well, as long as the GameType supports it. Since it started supporting mobile devices, UDK has provided a set of sequence objects that are targeted for the mobile platform.

Mobile Kismet – actions

Unlike the traditional UDK game that would require either changing `.ini` files or writing UnrealScript to accept and respond to input, UDK gives mobile developers the ability to do things how they want directly in Kismet. This allows developers to change input on a per-level basis.

Add Input Zone

Add Input Zone displays an additional input zone to the screen. Zones need to have a unique name and will be referenced by their **Zone Name** property in other sequence objects when using them. We will be using this action later in the chapter in order to add buttons to our UI and learn how to create different kinds of zones for use in our project.

This action is found in **NewAction | Mobile | AddInputZone**.

Clear Input Zone

This action removes all of the zones that were created or loaded at runtime. This basically leaves you with a clean slate to build an input scheme of your own. This is great if you are creating a game that does not require movement, or uses a different way of moving than what the provided ones do.

This action is found in **NewAction | Mobile | ClearInputZones**.

 Using this action would also remove the **UberStickMoveZone** and **UberStickLookZone** joystick inputs leaving only the **UberLookZoneInput** zone left. Be sure to add them back if you'd like to have them within your project. However, that being said, it is likely best for users to avoid using this Event unless it is for a specific purpose within a single level. If we don't want parts of the default input zones for all levels, it is best that we modify the **RequiredMobileInputConfigs** of the DefaultGameUDK.ini file to fit our purposes.

Remove Input Zone

This action allows you to remove an input zone by name; it is useful if you want to make an interaction only available at certain times of a game, like a save menu or a **Talk** button used for dialog. The **Zone Name** property can be found within the properties of the sequence object.

This action is found in **NewAction | Mobile | RemoveInputZone**.

Save/Load values

This, as the name suggests, saves or loads variables created within Kismet from the hard drive using Kismet. You can hook up multiple variables to the same action allowing you to have as many variables as you like, but each variable needs to have a name within the **Var Name** property to be saved. I recommend that you use the same action for both loading and saving the same values. This way the order in which the variables are loaded are the same in which they were saved. If you have ten integers hooked to the same **Int Vars** holder Kismet does not guarantee the order in which it decides to place it and using the same action saves you the headache.

This action is found in **NewAction | Mobile | Save/LoadValues**.

Mobile Kismet – events

Taking the input from input zones, as well as the iPod's own gyroscopes and gadgets, we can make use of certain functionality with events, as well as create our own **HUD** graphics.

Analog Input

Working on PC, Console, and Mobile, **Analog Input** will fire whenever an analog input, used with the **Input Name** that you set with, has a value.

Some values that you can use include `MobileYaw` and `MobilePitch` which give values from the device's gyroscope. These will give you float values inside of the **Float Value** variable. **DeviceAccelerometerRawData** will return a vector with the `Roll`, `Portrait Pitch`, and `Landscape Pitch` in the **Vector Value** variable.

It is important to note that unless you set **Trap** input to **FALSE** (by unchecking it), nothing else will be able to receive any input events, including touches.

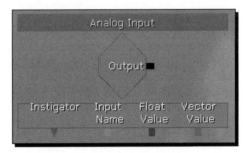

This action is found in **New Event | Input | AnalogInput**.

Mobile Button Access

If you are not referencing something that was already created from a `.ini` file, you will be using **Mobile Button Access** to trigger stuff within Kismet. This is similar to how the **Touch** event was shown previously. The property **Target Zone Name** should contain the name of an already created input zone. There are some properties that you can use, such as **Send Press Only On Touch Down** which will only call the **Input Pressed Output** when you click on the button and **Send Press Only On Touch Up** which will only be called when you remove your finger. Otherwise, as long as the button is held down, the action will be called.

This action is found in **New Event | Input | Mobile Button Access**.

Mobile Input Access

The Mobile Input Access action is used whenever you have an input zone set with the value of **Mobile Input Zone** to **ZoneType_Joystick**. **Input Active** is called in each frame when the joystick is being used, while **Input Inactive** is used when it is released. Creating variables for the bottom sections gives you access to different values that you can use for interpreting how you are going to use the data. **X-Axis** and **Y-Axis** give you a value between **-1.0** and **1.0**, where **-1.0** is all the way down or left, and **1.0** is up or right. If you would prefer to be more precise, the four other values give you the pixel values of where the joystick's center and current position are.

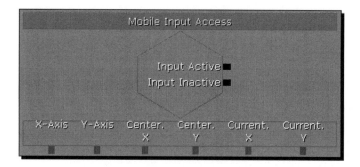

This action is found in **New Event | Input | MobileInputAccess**.

Mobile Look

Mobile Look is extremely similar to the **Mobile Input Access** event, in that they both have the same type of outputs and are used with an input zone with **ZoneType_Joystick** as the **Mobile Input Zone**. However, the **Mobile Look** action takes the data and converts it into a Vector that represents the current vertical and horizontal axes of the joystick, instead of individual values which can be easily applied to a pawn using **New Action | Actor | Set Actor Location**. The **Yaw** represents the direction the joy stick is moving in **Unreal Rotator** units where **0** is straight up and the rotation increases clockwise. The **Strength** gives the distance of the current location of the touch to the center of the joystick in pixels. This can be quite useful for top-down games.

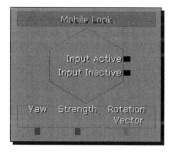

This action is found in **New Event | Input | Mobile Look**.

Mobile Object Picker

Mobile Object Picker is a simple way to check if target object with collision is being touched by a **Touch** input if it is within the **Trace Distance** away from the player. It will only call once unless you set **Check on Touch** to **TRUE**, then it will call once every frame. Like everything that does an action every frame, it is advised to set a **Re Trigger Delay** to some value such as 0.2 in order to put less strain on the hardware.

This action is found in **New Event | Input | Mobile Object Picker**.

Mobile Simple Swipes

The **Mobile Simple Swipes** event provides a simplistic form of swipe detection using different outputs depending on the swipe's direction. The **Tolerance** variable can be set to allow a swipe to occur on a more or less straight line and the **Min Distance** variable sets how long the swipe needs to be to be considered a swipe to make the move more or less drastic. The bottom value in purple, **Touched Actors List,** returns an object list which contains all of the actors with collision that were touched in the process of the swipe.

This action is found in **New Event | Input | Mobile Simple Swipes**.

Touch Input

Any time the user touches the screen, it is considered a **Touch** event. The input system has the ability to track multiple touches at the same time by using the **Touch Index** with the **Touchpad Index** to refer to the input zone values that you provided. **Touch X** and **Touch Y** will give you the value in pixels of where in screen space they are and **Instigator** will refer to the **Player Controller** that did the touching. You may choose to use **Pressed** for a triggered event with **Repeated** to continue while the touch exists. **Released** will be called whenever the player removes his finger from the **Touch** event.

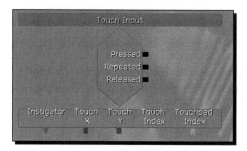

This action is found in **New Event | Input | Touch Input**.

 Unless you set **Trap Input** to **FALSE** by unchecking it, you will be unable to use any other input zones while using this event.

Draw Image

The **Draw Image** action displays the **Texture2D** image in **Display Texture** as a **HUD** of sorts for players to use within your game as long as **Active/Is Active** are set to be **TRUE**. The **XL** and **YL** values are used to show how large the image should be to display **1.0** means to fill the screen 100% within the respective axis. **U** and **L** are the location of the top-left corner of that texture to draw. **UL** and **VL** are the horizontal and vertical width in pixels of the portion of the texture to be drawn. Make sure to change the **Display Color** to white as that is the color that it will be modulated by.

There is a variable called **Authored Global Scale,** which specifies the scale factor of the display the content is being used in. A value of 2.0 is useful for high resolution screens like the iPhone 4S and new iPad, while 1.0 is useful for standard resolution screens such as the iPad and older iPhones/iPod Touches. It is also worth noting that the **Out** output does not actually get called.

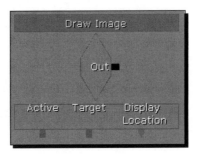

This action is found in **New Event | HUD | Draw Image**.

 This will not work with the gametype of **UTDeathmatch**. We will make use of this for our Main Menu, which we will be creating in *Chapter 7, Advanced Content Creation for Urban Warrior*.

Draw Text

This event will display a string of text provided by **Display Text** on the screen. Be sure to set a value for **Display Font** using one of the fonts provided in the **Content Browser**. There are two **Text Draw Method** choices in how the text is going to be drawn on the screen; **DRAW_CenterText** which centers the text horizontally from the **Display Location** variable and **DRAW_WrapText** which draws the text wrapped starting from the **Display Location**. The text will be displayed as long as **Active/Is Active** are set to **TRUE**. The **Target** is the player that we want this information to be displayed to and will typically be the Player.

Like our **Draw Image** event, there is a variable called **Authored Global Scale** which specifies the scale factor of the display the content is being used in. A value of **2.0** is useful for high resolution screens like the iPhone 4S and new iPad, while **1.0** is useful for standard resolution screens such as the iPad and older iPhones/iPod Touches. It is also worth noting that the **Out** output does not actually get called.

 This will not work with the gametype of **UTDeathmatch**. We will make use of this for our Main Menu, which we will be creating in *Chapter 7, Advanced Content Creation for Urban Warrior*.

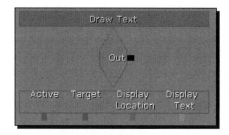

This action is found in **New Event | HUD | Draw Text**.

Give some input to the situation

With that basic overview of the different mobile-specific sequence objects, let's put that knowledge to some good use.

Time for action – adding input

Right now in our game, we use the two joysticks that are provided in order to move around and glance around the world. If you tap the middle of the screen, the gun will fire, but there are other things that players can do that are already pre-written into the gametype. With a few of the new Kismet sequence objects we have learned about, we are going to create buttons that will allow the player to shoot, use their alternative fire, and jump.

1. Open up the Kismet editor by pressing the **K** button.

2. Create an **Add Input Zone** action by right-clicking and selecting **New Action | Mobile | Add Input Zone**.

3. Expand the **Seq Act Mobile Add Input Zones** tab and set the value of **Zone Name** to **AltFire**.

4. Click on the blue triangle icon on the far end of **New Zone**, and then click on **MobileInputZone** to create a new zone we can use.

5. Expand the **Zone** tab and set the value of **Caption** to **AltFire**.

6. Expand the **Input** tab and set the value of **Input Key** to GBA_AltFire.

7. Expand the **Bounds** tab and set the value of **X** to **-100.0** and **Y** to **-300**.

The **X** and **Y** values of the bounds, if positive, will be moved from the top-left of the screen. Placing a negative number in either of the axes will cause the **HUD** to move the display to the bottom right-hand side edge of the viewport, which is what we want to achieve. We want to place our **HUD** buttons on the bottom right-hand side near the joystick used for glancing, so we use a negative number for each axis. Note that these values given were meant for the iPhone; they will need to be adjusted for use on other iOS devices.

8. Expand the **Rendering** tab and click on **Render Color**. Change it to some value that will be easily seen in your level. I picked blue for this level.

9. Copy the **Add Input Zone** action and paste two copies of them inside our Kismet workspace. In the first copy, change the **Zone Name** and **Caption** variables to **Jump** and set the **Input Key** to GBA_Jump with a position of (**-200, -350**) in the **Bounds**. For the second one, change the **Zone Name** and **Caption** variables to **Fire** and set the **Input Key** to GBA_Fire with a position of (**-300, -300**) in the **Bounds**.

10. From the **Out** output of the **Console Command** Mode, connect our **Add Input Zone** sequence objects one after the other.

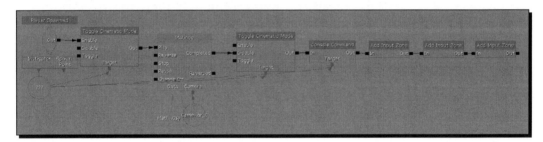

11. Save your project (**File | Save**) and start your game by clicking on the **Start Mobile Previewer** button on the main toolbar.

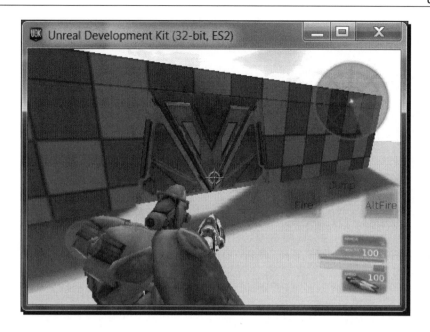

What just happened?

We've now created our own custom input buttons allowing us to jump, fire, and shoot our alternative fire while retaining the original movement options. This will be quite useful when we get new weapons such as the rocket launcher, or if we want to provide platforming of a sort to our game.

Have a go hero – mobile sequence objects / adding input

Using the sequence objects described previously, it would be very simple to create many different kinds of games, including a hidden object game, where you are given two images that are almost exactly the same, aside from a few differences. Upon touching one of the differences, it would be hidden and you'd be closer to finding all of them. Prototype this functionality by using the **Mobile Object Picker** event, and the **Toggle Hidden** action to hide the door object we created when you click on it.

Pop quiz

1. Which of the following is not a Kismet object type?

    a. Events

    b. Actions

    c. Console Command

    d. Conditions

2. What effect does changing the Max Trigger Count to 0 do?

    a. The event will be triggered an infinite amount of times.

    b. It is not used anymore but exists for backwards compatibility,
        so there is no effect.

    c. Tells UDK how many Trigger/Trigger Volume may exist in our level.

    d. The event will not be triggered until its value is larger.

3. What Kismet Event would I use to get information from the iOS device's gyroscope?

    a. Touch Input

    b. Analog Input

    c. Mobile Input Access

    d. Mobile Simple Swipes

4. How would I remove the two joysticks that are included in our gametype?

    a. Clear Input Zones

    b. Remove Input Zone for each joystick

    c. Modify the RequiredMobileInputConfigs of DefaultGameUDK.ini

    d. All of the above

5. What type of actor do we use in order to change the player's vision?

    a. Player Spawned

    b. Matinee

    c. VisionActor

    d. CameraActor

Summary

We learned a lot in this chapter about Unreal's advanced systems of Kismet in Matinee. We've implemented them both individually and together to see how they can be used to create a more interesting and dynamic experience within our game world. Using this fundamental knowledge, you can basically create any type of game you want; the possibilities are limitless!

In this short period of time, we've managed to cover quite a lot of things. We've specifically learned the following

- What Kismet is and how it can be used to create level-based events and prototyping
- How to call console commands at runtime allowing us to change to a third-person perspective
- What Kismet should be used for and reasons why we would or would not decide to use it
- How Matinee is the cinematic tool of the Unreal Engine and allows designers to give exact direction in how things work in the engine
- How to create an introductory cutscene bringing players into our world
- What the implementation of an automatic door using aspects of both Kismet and Matinee would look like
- How Kismet is different on the Mobile platform and the extra functionality we get from that
- How to add functionality missing from the gametype using Sequence Objects we discussed previously

Now that we've learned about the basics of Kismet and Matinee, we're ready to explore how we can take our knowledge of Kismet to the next level and begin taking more steps towards building our Urban Warrior project.

In the next chapter, we will be creating some dynamic action sequences by creating more complex systems, such as regenerating health (the console FPS favorite) and spawning enemies whose behavior and placement seem as realistic as possible.

5
Action Sequences for Urban Warrior

In the previous chapter, we built up a basic understanding of the lovely tools of Kismet and Matinee and how they can work together in some simple examples. But now that we know the basics can't we do more? Oh yes, we certainly can.

In this chapter we are going to create a series of sequences and prefabs to set the groundwork, allowing us to easily create our level in the next chapter.

In this chapter we shall:

◆ Discuss what sequences are and how we use them

◆ Spawn an enemy into our level

◆ Develop a rudimentary AI system that will shoot at us if we are close

◆ Expand upon that system by adding chasing and retreating behavior

◆ Import/export subsequences to create additional enemies easily

◆ Implement regenerating health using remote events

◆ Discuss prefabs and their use in our project

◆ Make a door prefab

◆ Discuss workflow and things to consider when creating combat scenarios

So with that, let's take a look at what we can do with sequences.

Sequences and you

Sequences are UDK's ways of helping you organize your code as well as compartmentalize all of the actions that you want to have happen in a certain area. Events and their associated actions, that you will be re-using, are also prime candidates for being placed inside sequences.

Anyone who works with Kismet has worked with sequences before. You have already been using sequences without even knowing it. UDK provides us with a **LevelName** sequence within the Kismet editor that we have used in the previous chapter.

Life, or something like it

Now that we have an idea of what sequences are, let's create one of our own! It will enable us to bring the characters to life, such as enemies, explained in this section.

Time for action – spawning AI into our level

As we are creating the building blocks of our game, creating a third person shooter is kind of hard to do without having enemies to fight. Thankfully UDK has helped us out and made it incredibly easy to add enemies into our level!

1. Go into to the **Actor Classes** browser **View | Browser Windows | Actor Classes**. From there you will see a list of classes that we can place within our level. Type Path in the **Search** bar and left-click on the **PathNode** selection. The following screenshot explains this:

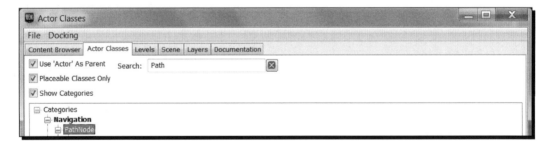

2. Close the **Actor Classes** browser and right-click anywhere in your level. From the menu that pops up select **Add PathNode Here**. This will create an actor on the ground on the spot where you clicked. I have placed my **PathNode** away from the player but still visible from the camera for our opening sequence.

3. Open the Kismet editor by clicking on the **K** icon at the top of the UDK interface on the main toolbar.

4. Left click-and-drag the background of the workspace to move the graph plane, bringing some open space for us to work with.

5. Right-click somewhere in the background and select **Create New Sequence: 0 Objs**. A pop-up window should come up asking you for the name of the sequence. Type `EnemyAI` and press *Enter*. A little box with the name should be created at the position where you right-clicked.

6. Double-click on the **EnemyAI** sequence. You will notice that we have now moved into this sequence and there is nothing there, and that our Sequences pane on the bottom at right-hand side has the **EnemyAI** sequence highlighted. This is shown in the following screenshot:

7. Right-click and create a **Sequence Activated** event by choosing **New Event | Sequence Activated** from the menu.

8. Create an **Actor Factory** action by right-clicking and choosing **New Action | Actor | Actor Factory** from the menu. Go into the Properties pane and click on the blue triangle on the right-hand side of the **Factory** variable and select **UTActorFactoryAI** from the pop-up menu that comes out to create a new **Actor Factory** to use. Inside our new factory's properties set the **Pawn Class** to **UTPawn** and check the **Give Default Inventory** option. Finally, change the **Team Index** to 1.

9. Underneath the **Spawn Point** variable create an external object variable by right-clicking and selecting **New Variable | External Variable** from the menu. Left-click on the variable and in its properties set **Expected Type** to **SeqVar_Object** and **Variable Label** to **Spawn Point**.

10. Create a **Finish Sequence** action by right-clicking and selecting **New Action | Misc | Finish Sequence**. Under the **Output Label** property type Spawned.

11. Connect the **Out** of the **Sequence Activated "In"** event to the **Spawn Actor** input of the Actor Factory action. Connect the **Spawn Point** link to the **External Object** variable we created. Finally, connect the **Finished** output of the **Actor Factory** to the **Finish Sequence "Spawned"** action. At this point our sequence should look as shown in the following screenshot:

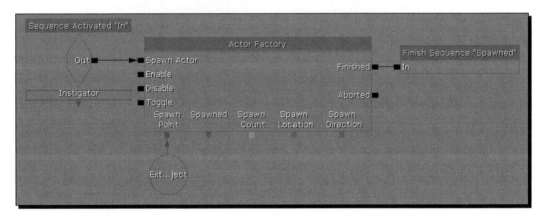

12. On the bottom right-hand side of our Kismet editor click on the **LevelName** sequence to return to the main level sequence. We should now see the sequence look similar to a Kismet node with inputs, outputs, and variable chains, as shown in the following screenshot:

13. Right-click and create a **Level Loaded** event by choosing **New Event | Level Loaded** from the menu.

14. Go into our level and left-click on the PathNode that you created earlier and go back into Kismet. Right-click on our Spawn Point link and select **Create New Variable from PathNode_0**. This is shown in the following screenshot:

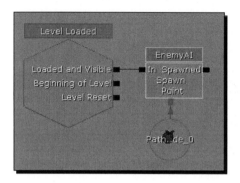

15. Build our game by selecting **Build | Build All** and pressing Close when finished.

16. Save your project. Now start your game by clicking on the **Start Mobile Previewer** button on the main toolbar as shown in following screenshot:

What just happened?

Upon the level being loaded (via the **Level Loaded** event) we call our **EnemyAI** sequence which spawns an enemy (via an **Actor Factory**) and places him in the level where our **PathNode** is. Putting these events and actions into a sequence will enable us to put code relevant to our AI in one place making it as simple as possible to create new AIs in our future levels.

It lives! but...

As you can now tell, our actor is in the level, but it isn't really doing anything. That is because it lacks **artificial intelligence (AI)**. Surely we could force the actor to use the **Deathmatch** AI that is included in UDK, but if we had more than one AI they would fight each other. One thing that experienced UDK developers may come to realize is that you lose a lot of functionality when making a game for iOS. For example, if we were creating the game on PC I could just use the `UTTeamGame` type which would take care of not attacking actors other than the player, but that functionality is broken if you were to use the iOS build. Fear not dear reader; I do have a solution and you'll learn about sequences and some advanced Kismet in the process!

Time for action – base enemy AI

Now we will be creating a rudimentary AI using Kismet and using our sequence we will be able to attach this behavior to every AI that we use.

1. Open the Kismet editor by clicking on the **K** icon at the top of the UDK interface on the main toolbar.

2. Enter the **EnemyAI** sequence by either double-clicking on the sequence in the **Graph** pane or clicking on the **EnemyAI** text in the **Sequences** pane.

3. Underneath the **Spawned** variable inside the **Actor Factory** create an external object variable by right-clicking and selecting **New Variable | External Variable** from the menu. Left-click on the variable and inside of its properties set **Expected Type** to **SeqVar_Object** and **Variable Label** to **Spawned**.

4. Create an **Is Alive** conditional by right-clicking and selecting **New Condition | Is Alive?** Connect the **Spawned** variable link to the **Players** link underneath the conditional.

5. Create a **Finish Sequence** action by right-clicking and selecting **New Action | Misc | Finish Sequence**. Under the **Output Label** property type `Dead`. Connect the **False** output of the **Is Alive** conditional to the **In** of the **Finish** sequence.

6. Create a **Trace** action by right-clicking and selecting **New Action | Misc | Trace**. Connect the **True** output of the **Is Alive** conditional to the In of the **Trace**. Connect the **Start** variable link on the bottom of the trace equal to the **Spawned** variable used previously. Set the **End** variable link to a **Player 0** variable (**New Variable | Player | Player** with **All Players** unchecked). Right-click under the **Distance** variable link and create a new Float variable. This is shown in the following screenshot:

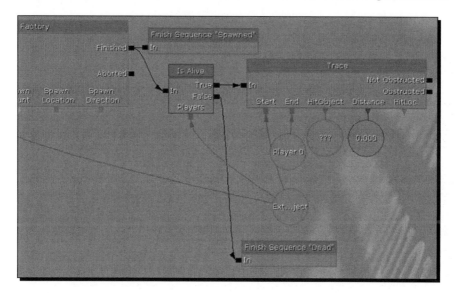

7. Create a **Compare Float** conditional by right-clicking and selecting **New Condition | Comparison | Compare Float**. Underneath the **A** variable link connect the variable under Distance in our trace. Underneath **B** create a new Float variable and enter a value of 600.

8. Create a **Start Firing At** action by right-clicking and selecting **New Action | AI | Start Firing At**. Set the **Target** variable to the Spawned object variable and the **Fire At** link to a **Player 0** object. Connect the **A < B** of the **Compare Float** conditional to the **In** of the **Start Firing At** action.

9. Create a **Stop Firing** action by right-clicking and selecting **New Action | AI | Stop Firing**. Set the **Target** variable to the Spawned object variable. Connect the **A >= B** of the **Compare Float** conditional to the In of the **Start Firing At** action. We will see the output as shown in the following screenshot:

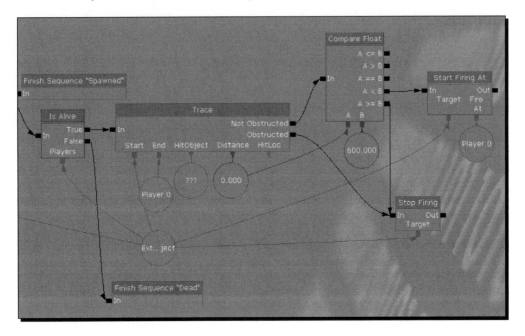

Now, if our enemy is alive, we will perform a trace on the screen which will create a line between the actor and the player and will see whether there is anything between them that would break **line-of-sight (LOS)**. If the AI can see the player and he's within a certain distance of the player, he will start firing at him. If something is in the way he will stop. Of course, right now this is only called once. So after it happens once it won't be called again. What if the player runs away from the fight? We want to have the enemy chase after the player.

10. Create a **Compare Bool** conditional by right-clicking and selecting **New Condition | Comparison | Compare Bool**. Underneath the Bool variable link create a **Bool** variable with a **False** value.

11. Create a **Move To Actor** action by right-clicking and selecting **New Action | AI | Move To Actor**. Underneath the **Target** variable link connect the Spawned object. Under **Destination** create a Player variable and connect it. Connect the **True** output from the **Compare Bool** conditional to the In input on the **Move To Actor** action.

12. Create a **Toggle** action by right-clicking and selecting **New Action | Toggle | Toggle**. Underneath the **Bool** variable link connect the **Bool** variable we created earlier with `False` as the value. Connect the Out output of the **Start Firing At** action to the **Turn On** input of this **Toggle** action.

13. Create a **Delay** action by right-clicking and selecting **New Action | Misc | Delay**. In the **Properties** pane change the **Duration** to `0.20`. Connect the **Out** from the **Toggle** and **Move to Actor** actions as well as the **False** output from the Compare Bool conditional to the **Start** input of our **Delay**. Connect the **Finished** output of our **Delay** action to the **In** of the **Is Alive** conditional we created at the beginning of this section.

14. Build our game by selecting **Build | Build All** and pressing **Close** when finished.

15. Save your project and start your game by clicking on the **Start Mobile Previewer** button on the main toolbar as shown in the following screenshot:

What just happened?

Our enemy now responds to what we do in the world! If we come within a distance of `600` or closer to the enemy, and it has a clear line-of-sight, it will start firing at us. If the player runs a certain distance away or goes behind some cover, it will attempt to travel to us. However there is still a lot of work to do.

Improvements to be made

Instead of running to the player's position, the enemy we spawned goes towards the spawn point, or rather the place where the character was initially created, rather than where they currently are. It will continue to follow delete us, until it can fire at us again as well. Shouldn't it give up after a while? If we start attacking the enemy at a distance, the player will not react and will just take hits as well. With this basis, we can now extend our AI to be much more robust.

Time for action – base enemy AI

Now we will be creating a rudimentary AI using Kismet and using our sequence we will be able to attach this behavior to every AI that we use.

1. Go into the **Actor Classes** browser **View | Browser Windows | Actor Classes**. From there, you will see a list of classes that we can place within our level. Type `Path` in the **Search** bar and left-click on the **PathNode_Dynamic** selection. The following screenshot shows this:

2. Close the **Actor Classes** browser and right-click anywhere in your level. From the menu that pops up, select **Add PathNode_Dynamic Here**. This will create an actor on the ground in the spot where you clicked. Place it nearby the player's spawn point.

3. Open the Kismet editor by clicking on the **K** icon at the top of the UDK interface on the main toolbar.

4. Enter the **EnemyAI** sequence by either double-clicking on the sequence in the **Graph** pane or clicking on the **EnemyAI** text in the **Sequences** pane.

5. Delete the connections to the **Start** input on the **Delay** action by holding *Alt* and clicking on the black square. Left-click on the **Delay** action, hold *Shift* and drag it to the right-hand side to give some room for our new additions.

6. Select the **Move to Actor** action and its attached variables by holding down
Ctrl + Alt and left-clicking slightly above and to the left-hand side of the **Move to
Actor** action, and drag until the box you create covers all of the items we want to
move. Alternatively, hold *Ctrl* and click on each item. Move the objects to beside the
Delay position. Delete the connection from the **In** of the **Move To Actor** action and
connect the **Out** from the **Move To Actor** action to the **Start** of the **Delay** action.
Connect the **Out** of our **Toggle** action to the **Start** of the **Delay** action.

7. Create a **Compare Float** conditional next to our **Compare Bool** action by
right-clicking and selecting **New Condition | Conditional | Compare Float**.
Connect the **True** of the **Compare Bool** conditional to the **In** input of this **Compare
Float**. Connect the **False** output of the **Compare Bool** to the **Start** input on the
Delay action. Create a float variable in both the **A** and **B** section of our **Compare
Float** action. Inside the **A** float variable, create a comment saying **timeSinceCaught**
with a value of 0.0. Set the **B** variable to have a value of 2.0. What I'm trying to
accomplish in this section, is making it so that if the AI chases after the player and
a certain time passes, he will give up and stop where he is.

8. Create an **Add Float** action by right-clicking and selecting **New Action | Math |
Add Float**. Connect the **A** and **Float Result** variables of **Add Float** action to the float
variable that we placed a comment saying **timeSinceCaught,** which is connected to
the **A** link on our **Compare Float**. Connect the **A < B** output of our **Compare Float** to
the **In** of our **Add Float** action. Create a float variable below **B** with a value of 0.2.
The following screenshot shows this:

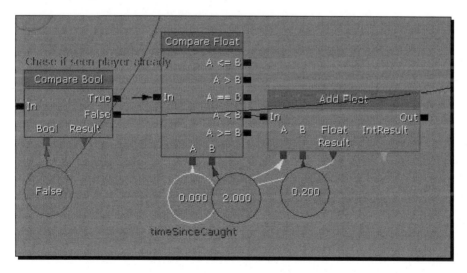

As this action is called every 0.2 seconds (due to our delay), we add 0.2 to our counter if it has been less than 2 seconds since we started chasing the player after seeing them for the first time. What do we do if we have waited 2 seconds or more? That's what we're going to do next.

9. Below the **Add Float** action we just created add a **Set Float** action by using **New Action | Set Variable | Float**. Create a new float with a value of 0.0 for the **Value** link and connect the **Target** variable to the **timeSinceCaught** float variable. Connect the **A >= B** output from the **Compare Float** conditional to the **In** of our **Set Float** action.

10. Create a **Toggle** action by right-clicking and selecting **New Action | Toggle | Toggle**. Underneath the **Bool** variable link connect the **Bool** variable we created earlier with **False** value. Connect the **Out** output of the **Set Float** action to the **Turn Off** input of this **Toggle** action.

11. Create a **Modify Property** action by using **New Action | Object Property | Modify Property**. Go to the **Properties** pane and left-click on the green + sign beside the **Properties** variable, to create a new property to change. Click on the black triangle on the left-hand side to expand the options. Inside the **Property Name** property type bLockLocation. Click on the checkbox for **Modify Property**. Finally, in the **Property Value** section type 1. This is shown in the following screenshot:

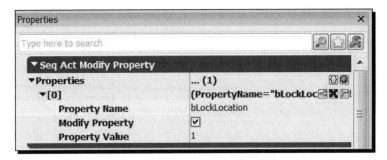

The **bLockLocation** variable is a **Bool** contained within our **Actor** class that will prevent an actor from being moved. With a value other than 0, a **Bool** will treat the value to mean true which will freeze our AI until we set the value back to 0. Note that UDK will give us a warning about using the **Modify Property** action, but as we are not going to be using UnrealScript for our project it will be fine.

12. Connect the **Out** from the **Toggle** action to the **In** of our **Modify Property** action. Connect the **Target** to the **Spawned** external variable. Connect the **Out** output of the **Modify Property** action to the **Start** on our **Delay** action on the far right-hand side.

13. Next to the **Add Float** that we created in step 8 create a **Modify Property** action by using **New Action | Object Property | Modify Property**. Go to the **Properties** pane and left-click on the green **+** sign beside the **Properties** variable to create a new property to change. Click on the black triangle on the left-hand side to expand the options. Inside the **Property Name** property type bLockLocation. Click on the checkbox for **Modify Property**. Finally, in the **Property Value** section type 0. Connect the **Out** output of the **Add Float** action to the **In** of our new **Modify Property** action.

14. Go back into the editor and confirm that you have the **PathNode_Dynamic_0** selected.

15. Back in Kismet create a **Get Location and Rotation** action **New Action | Actor | Get Location and Rotation**. Set the **Target** variable to **Player 0** by creating a player object variable. Right-click under the **Location** link and select **Create New Vector Variable**.

16. Delete the **Player** variable under the **Move to Actor** action and right-click under the **Destination** variable and select **New Object Var using PathNode_Dynamic_0**. Create a **Set Actor Location** action **New Action | Actor | Set Actor Location**. Connect the **Location** variable link to the location that we created in the previous step. Connect the **Target** of the **Set Actor Location** action to the **Destination** variable link on the **Move to Actor**.

17. Above our **Trace** action create a **Take Damage** event by right-clicking and selecting **New Event | Actor | Take Damage**. In the **Properties** pane set **Max Trigger Count** to 0. Connect the **Instigator** to the **Spawned** object. Connect the **Out** output to the **In** input of the **Start Firing At** action.

    This will make it so that if the player decides to attack someone from far away, that the enemy will react in some way by chasing after the player. Finally we will see something similar to the following screenshot:

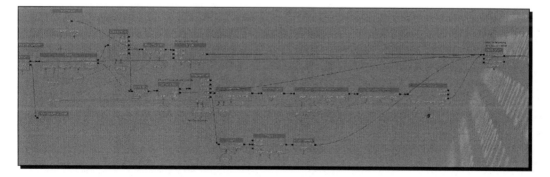

18. Back in the editor window, click on the **Door** we created in the previous chapter. Open its properties by pressing *F4* and type `path` in the search box. You will see a box checked for the value **Path Colliding**. Uncheck it. Unchecking the **Path Colliding** value lets the editor know that it is possible for AI to pass through the door, as it will treat the area as being open even though we have a door there. If you intend to not allow enemies to use doors then you'd want to make sure this is checked.

19. Build our game by selecting **Build | Build All** and pressing **Close** when finished.

20. Save your project and start your game by clicking on the **Start Mobile Previewer** button on the main toolbar as shown in following screenshot:

What just happened?

We breathed much more life into the routines of our AIs; they are now reacting to us in a much more believable way, and are good enough for what we are doing in our project. Now the enemies will chase to where you are for a period of time, giving up after a while, and if you attack them from anywhere, they will react to you. We've also been exposed to much more advanced Kismet scripting, showing us how we can manipulate the game environment based on events happening in the world.

Have a go hero – taking your AI further

There are plenty of other things that you can add to your AI, such as different states depending on how close the player is to them (distance of the **Trace** action was discussed in the *Base enemy AI* section). Right now as long as the **timeSinceCaught** variable is less than 2.0, the `PathNode_Dynamic` is set to your actual position as well. You could make it so that the AI could only know where you were at that point (only setting the position once). You can use the **Bool** (true/false statement) the variable red in color as a way of checking whether it was already set or not.

Another thing that you can do is use a **Timer** (**Action | Misc | Timer**) rather than using float comparisons and addition, toggling a timer on and off as necessary to add one other tool to your toolbox.

Exporting subsequences

After setting up a useful subsequence such as our **EnemyAI** event that we created, we may want to share it between other levels. One way to do this is just copy/pasting; but what if we want to share our sequence with other developers/designers or on different computers? One of the neat things that we can do with sequences is export them so that we can place them inside our levels much in the same way that we place meshes or **Actor Classes**. One thing to note though is that when a sequence is imported it will remove all references to objects within the level that was created, so for that reason having external variables for items is vital to make sure that the sequence performs the way we'd like it to.

Time for action – creating a second enemy

At this point, it's a good idea to save our **EnemyAI** subsequence as we are going to use it inside our final level. As this is the first time we've exported something to the content editor, I'm going to be very thorough.

1. Go into to the **Actor Classes** browser **View | Browser Windows | Actor Classes**. From there you will see a list of classes that we can place within our level. Type `Path` in the **Search** bar and left-click on the **PathNode** selection.

2. Close the **Actor Classes** browser and right-click in front of the door we created in the previous chapter. From the menu that pops up, select **Add PathNode Here**. Select the **PathNode**, hold **Option** and drag the object behind the door, creating a copy.

3. Open the Kismet editor by clicking on the **K** icon at the top of the UDK interface on the main toolbar.

4. Right-click on our **EnemyAI** subsequence and select **Export Sequence to Package**. This is shown in the following screenshot:

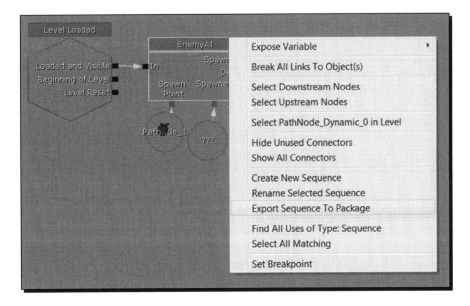

5. A prompt will come up asking for the package, group, and name of your object. Under **Package** put `UrbanWarrior`, in **Group** put `Sequences`, and under **Name** put `EnemyAI`.

6. Open up the **Content Browser**, and in the **Search** bar underneath **Packages** type `urban`. You should see your package come up on top with your sequence being the first item selected.

7. Right-click on the package (it should have a * next to it) and click on **Save**. This is shown in the following screenshot:

8. Left-click on the **EnemyAI** sequence and open up the Kismet editor. Move to the left-hand side of our **EnemyAI** sequence, right-click and select **Import EnemyAI Sequence**.

You may not see anything change, but there is a good reason for that.

9. Left-click on the **EnemyAI** subsequence and move it by holding *Alt* and dragging it to the left-hand side. You will notice that the new subsequence that we imported has the same position as when we exported it.

10. Left-click on the **PathNode** behind where the player is and go back into Kismet. Underneath the **Spawn Point,** right-click and select **New Object Var using PathNode_2 Here**. Create a new **Object** variable for the **Spawned** variable link. Connect the **Dead** output from the first **EnemyAI** sequence up to the **In** input of this **EnemyAI**.

Make sure at this point that your original and new **EnemyAI** sequences are both connected to the variable links that they need to be connected to as this is the point that most will probably have a problem.

11. Create a **Move To Actor** action by right-clicking and selecting **New Action | AI | Move To Actor**. Underneath the **Target** variable link connect the **Spawned** object. Under **Destination** connect it to the **PathNode** in front of the door. Connect the **Spawned** output from the **EnemyAI** subsequence to the **In** input on the **Move To Actor** action. We will see the output as shown in the following screenshot:

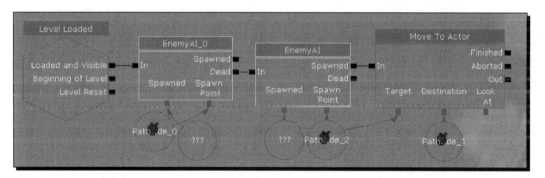

12. Build our game by selecting **Build | Build All** and pressing **Close** when finished.

13. Save your project and start your game by clicking on the **Start Mobile Previewer** button on the main toolbar, as shown in the following screenshot:

What just happened?

The world is becoming more and more dynamic. By using an imported subsequence we made it so that if our first enemy died, a second enemy would spawn and rush through the door to see what was going on.

Remote events

As seen in the previous sequence that we created, Kismet can often get quite complex and over time may become quite jumbled up. One possible solution to stop stay connections going all over the place is to use **Remote Events**. Similarly to our **Level Loaded** or **Player Spawned** events, whenever we activate a remote event through the **Activate Remote Event** Kismet action the actions and conditionals connected to it are called.

When we can use a remote event

Remote events sound quite amazing, but they can't always be used. Each remote event needs to have a specific name and UDK will get confused if you have multiple versions of the same remote event. This is also why we cannot have variables with the same name. If you are planning on re-using the same sequence for multiple objects, you cannot use them.

Creating a remote event

To create a **Remote Event** you right-click inside the **Graph** pane in Kismet and select **New Event | Remote Event**. After creating the event, go into its **Properties** and under the **Event Name** variable type a unique identifier. When you want the actions associated with the Remote Event to be called you just need to create an **Activate Remote Event** action **New Action | Event | Activate Remote Event** and in the **Properties** pane find the variable **Event Name** and set it to that same identifier. This is shown in the following screenshot:

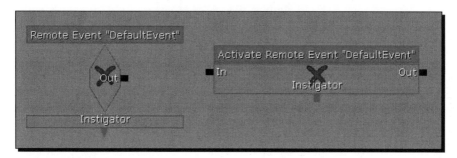

Named variables

In programming there is such a thing as global variables. **Global variables** are things that you wish to have at all times within the game; for example, a player's gold or the number of enemies currently spawned. This can be very useful if it's a piece of data that you use quite often. **Named variables** are basically Kismet's version of global variables; however, they are only global in terms of the level currently loaded.

When we can use a named variable

A **named variable,** just like a remote event, needs to have unique names which is why we used a comment instead of a variable name for our **timeSinceCaught** variable in our **EnemyAI** sequence. The nice thing about having variables with names is that instead of creating links to the one variable every single time, like we did with the **Spawned** external variable in our **EnemyAI** sequence, we can just create new named variables to hook it up to make our script much more organized.

Creating a named variable

To create a named variable you right-click inside the **Graph** pane in Kismet and select **New Variable | Named Variable**. After creating the variable and going into its properties you can set the expected type to what it is and under the **Find Var Name** property just fill in the variable name.

If everything goes correctly, you'll see a green checkmark in its position as shown in the following screenshot:

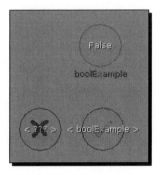

Manipulating the player

We have worked in such a way to create actions that work with the AIs we are going to place within the world, but there is one thing in the game that is more important that we haven't worked on yet at all: the player! Adding new types of gameplay or new mechanics are often tested out in Kismet before writing in UnrealScript, making it a lot easier to iterate. Make sure that the mechanics are? fun and interesting. Now that we have someone to shoot at us and some smarts, let's add a new mechanics to our player.

Time for action – regenerating player health over time

Made popular in *Halo* and seen in hit games such as *Gears of War* and *Batman: Arkham City*, regenerating health is a modern game mainstay that features in many *games* and are here to stay. Surprisingly, it is not that difficult at all to implement within Kismet, and you may notice some overlap between the behavior we use here and what we did previously.

1. Open the Kismet editor and enter our main sequence and drag the screen till you have a large amount of open space.

2. Create a remote event by selecting **New Event | Remote Event**. In the **Properties** pane set the **Event Name** variable to `RegenHealth`.

    Note that at this point you may see a large red **X** inside both of these icons; this means that since the last time it was refreshed, there is no remote event with that name or **Activate Remote Event** action to connect to it.

3. Directly above the remote event create a **Level Loaded** event by right-clicking and selecting **New Event | Level Loaded**.

4. To the right of the **Level Loaded** event create an **Activate Remote Event** action by right-clicking and selecting **New Action | Event | Activate Remote Event**. In the **Properties** pane find the variable **Event Name** and set it to RegenHealth.

Note that both the **Activate Remote Event** and remote event **RegenHealth** may still have a large red **X** in them. This is either due to a misspelling, or the sequence has not been refreshed. If you exit and enter Kismet again, you will see both of the objects have a green checkmark next to them as shown in the following screenshot:

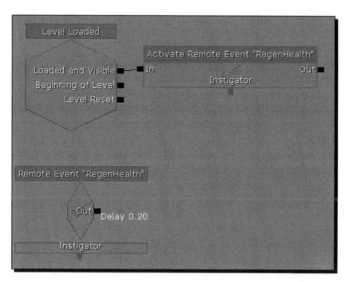

5. To the right-hand side of the remote event **RegenHealth** create a **Get Property** action by right-clicking and selecting **New Action | Object Property | Get Property**. In the **Properties** pane set the **Property Name** variable to Health. Underneath the **Target** variable link create a **Player 0** object variable. Underneath the **Int** variable link create a new **Int** variable by right-clicking underneath it and selecting **Create New Int Variable**.

Inside the UnrealScript file for the **Player** in the **Pawn Class** there exists an integer that has the name of **Health** which stores the player's health. The **Get Property** action allows us to see the value that it contains in our target, if it contains that variable.

6. Create a **Compare Int** conditional by right-clicking and selecting **New Condition |
Comparison | Compare Int**. Underneath the **A** variable link connect the variable
under **Int** in our **Get Property**. Underneath **B** create a new **Int** variable and put a
value of 100. Connect the **Out** from the **Get Property** action to the **In** input of the
Compare Int conditional.

Basically, we're going to compare whether our **Health** is lower than **100**
(the maximum value it can be at the moment) or not.

7. Create a **Modify Property** action by using **New Action | Object Property | Modify
Property**. Go to the **Properties** pane and left-click on the green **+** sign beside the
Properties variable to create a new property to change. Click on the black triangle
on the left-hand side to expand the options. Inside the **Property Name** property
type Health. Click on the checkbox for **Modify Property**. Finally, in the **Property
Value** section type 100. Under the **Target** variable link place a **Player 0** object.
Connect the **A >= B** from the **Compare Int** conditional to the **In** of the **Modify
Property** that we just created.

8. Create a **Compare Float** conditional by right-clicking and selecting **New Condition
| Comparison | Compare Float**. Underneath the **A** variable link create a new
Float variable and put a value of 0.0 with the **Var Name** of **TimeSinceDamaged**.
Underneath **B** create a new **Float** variable with a Float Value of 2.0 and **Obj
Comment of TimeSinceLastDamaged**. Connect the **A < B** output of the **Compare Int**
conditional to the **In** input of this **Compare Float** conditional.

9. Add a **Set Float** action by using **New Action | Set Variable | Float**. Create a new float
with a value of 0.0 for the **Value** link.

10. Create a named variable with an **Expected Type of SeqVar_Float** and a **Find Var
Name of TimeSinceDamaged** and connect the **Target** variable link from the **Set Float**
action to it. Connect the **Out** of the **Modify Property** (**Health**) to the **In** input of our
Set Float action.

11. Create an **Activate Remote Event** action **New Action | Event | Activate Remote Event** and in the **Properties** pane, find the variable **Event Name** and set it to **RegenHealth**. Connect the **Out** output of our **Set Float** action to the **In** of our **Activate Remote Event** variable **RegenHealth**. This is shown in the following screenshot:

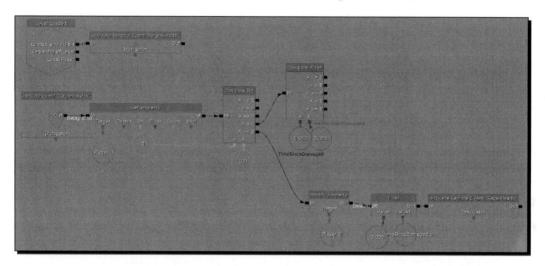

12. Create a **Modify Health** action **New Action | Actor | Modify Health**. Under the **Target** variable link create a **Player 0** object variable. Under amount create a **Float** variable with a value of 1.0. Inside the **Properties** pane check the **Heal** checkbox and connect the **A >= B** from our **Compare Float** conditional to the **In** of this action.

You may notice that we are not using **Modify Property** like we did in the previous example; this is merely to show you that there are often multiple ways of doing the exact same thing within Kismet and by experimenting you can discover all sorts of things that you can do.

13. Copy (*Ctrl + C*) and Paste (*Ctrl + V*) the **Activate Remote Event** variable **RegenHealth** that we created earlier. Drag the action till it is beside the **Modify Health** action we just created. Delete this one's connection to its **In** input by left-clicking while holding the *Alt* key. Copy and paste another one with the **In** removed and place it above this one. Hook the **Out** from our **Modify Health** to the one beside it.

14. Create an **Add Float** action by right-clicking and selecting **New Action | Math | Add Float**. Connect the **A** and **Float Result** variables of **Add Float** to a named variable with the value of **TimeSinceDamaged** like we did in step 10. Connect the **A < B** output of our **Compare Float** to the **In** of our **Add Float** action. Create a **Float** variable below **B** with a value of 0.2. Finally, connect the **Out** output of this **Add Float** to the extra **Activate Remote Event** variable **RegenHealth** we created in the previous step.

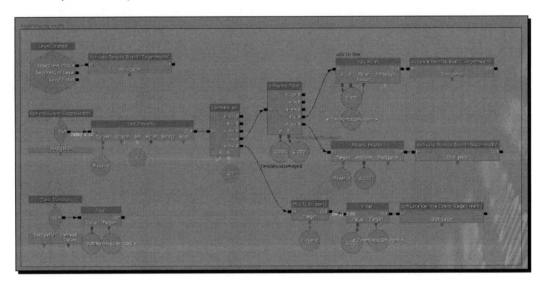

15. Save your project and start your game by clicking on the **Start Mobile Previewer** button on the main toolbar as shown in the following screenshot:

What just happened?

You can't tell by a still image, but we're one step closer to having a fully featured game, with the fantastic addition of a regenerating health system. When our health is not at maximum, we wait for a period of time and if we are not hit within that time period, we will slowly increase our health over time. We've also gained a good knowledge of how to use named variables, getting and setting object properties in Kismet, as well as experience in using remote events.

Have a go hero – regenerating player health over time

With this base system, there are plenty of things that you can do to extend the functionality. It would be easy to do something similar to *Halo's* shield recovery, by having the recovery go faster than the lower health you have, by changing the float value under the **Modify Health** action. You could also use the same sequence with a few changes to make it into something that will damage you if you spend too much time in it like with the water in *Sonic: The Hedgehog*.

Prefabs

Quite often when constructing a level, you want to create some arrangement of actors and associated Kismet, and then re-use that collection in the same or other levels, like the door we created. Prefabs allow you to create an object once, and then save it in a package as a prefab. You can then select the **Prefab** in the **Content Browser**, and add it as many times as you like throughout the level.

Note that prefabs can cause problems in UDK and may break and/or stop working for seemingly no reason so SAVE OFTEN after making sure that things work.

Time for action – door prefab

Right now we have one single door, and while it is an awesome door, we would probably like to have more than one inside our game. To make it easier to work with and place in new areas of our game, let's make a door prefab!

1. In Kismet, go to the door behavior that we wrote in the previous chapter. Hold *Alt+Ctrl* and drag from the top left-hand side of the objects to the bottom, to select all of the items used in the creation. Right-click and select **Create New Sequence**. In the following menu name the sequence Door. This is shown in the following screenshot:

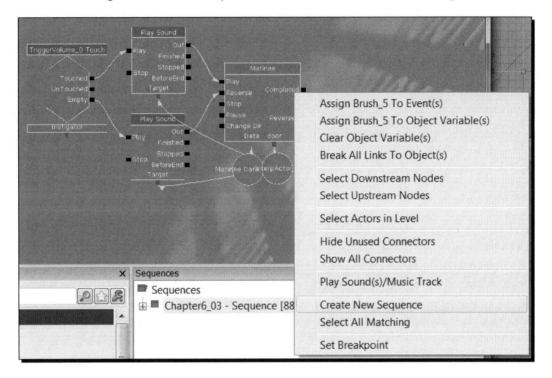

2. Similarly in the regular editor window, select all of the objects used to create our door, including the walls surrounding it and the trigger volume used in its creation. Right-click and select **Create Prefab**.

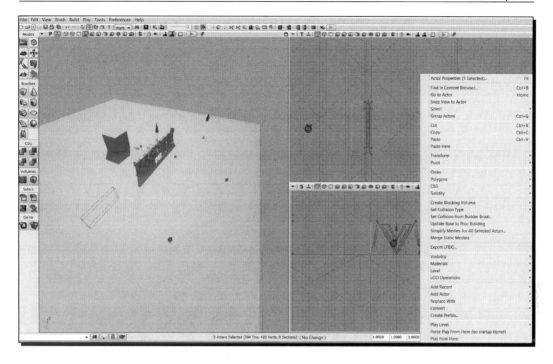

3. In the popup that is created under **Packages** use the name `UrbanWarrior` and inside the **Name** use `Door`.

4. Another popup will come up telling you that it detected a Kismet sequence using items of this prefab and wants to confirm that we want it to be part of the prefab. Click on **Yes**.

   Note that a prefab can only have one sequence associated with it, and you cannot use the main sequence as your sequence that uses that prefab. Unlike the subsequences that we exported/imported earlier, these objects will have the variable links in the sequence corresponding to the new copies made inside the prefab, which is a really neat thing.

5. Finally the popup will ask if you'd like to convert your door to an instance of the prefab; this is a good idea so click on **Yes**. You will now notice a red **P** symbol next to our door letting us know that it is a prefab.

6. Left-click on the prefab object and hold *Alt* while dragging it along an axis to create a copy of the door a distance away from the base point. You should see a second prefab being created and moved, as you drag along making another door in the process.

7. The walls will not appear inside the perspective view until you build the game, due to it not being able to render changes in BSP at runtime.

8. Build our game by selecting **Build | Build All** and pressing **Close** when finished.

9. Save your project and start your game by clicking on the **Start Mobile Previewer** button on the main toolbar, saying **Yes** when it asks you to save the package. The following screenshot shows the modified views:

What just happened?

We have now quickly and easily created a second door inside our level. The same functionality included in our previous door is still there, allowing us to enter and exit through both of them quite easily with the sound effects and everything. Using the prefab, it will be trivial to make new doors, and as they aren't forced to be the same (like Unity) we can change anything about each individual prefab without worrying about how it will affect the others.

Building combat sequences

As someone who enjoys playing games can attest to, there are always moments in gameplay that stand out from others. We've also played games where it just seemed that you were going through corridor after corridor, with little to no exciting things happening, with the game turning into a bore. Crafting a satisfying combat experience is something that every designer strives to do, and here are some suggestions on my end as to ways of doing just that.

Layouts

By failing to prepare, you are preparing to fail. - Benjamin Franklin

A good layout is the basis of a solid foundation for the creation of your level, and as such is probably the most important thing to consider when beginning a level. This is one of the numerous reasons why pre-production on game projects is so important. It may go against your initial thoughts, but it is not a good idea to just go in the editor and try to make something. While every once in a while you may stumble into something, it is far more likely that if you plan something out that the resulting level will be much better. That's not to say that what you plan in pre-production will be the same as how you planned it. Playtesting your level may teach you that certain things in the layout are confusing and/or too easy or hard which are important things to take note of. One of the most important things to keep in mind when working on a layout is making it easy to read at a first glance. Keep action in the player's **field of view** (FOV) when creating action.

You may have already noticed how in our current version of our layout our door is not in the player's view when spawned, making it confusing to where the player should continue in the game. This sends mixed signals, which is never a good thing.

Spawning and enemy placement

Of course, having a great layout is good, but if there is nothing to do in the environment, players will soon grow bored and as such we spawn opponents to face them. It is terribly important that enemies get spawned out of sight of the player, because seeing an enemy suddenly appear out of nowhere will suddenly break the suspension of disbelief that our player should be feeling, unless of course it is known as an ability of an enemy such as the Houdini splicers in *Bioshock*.

Of course, we also don't always want our enemies to be static; which is why we will often have enemies walking according to a path, or coming in from an area. This movement should give our player a visual cue, as just like the real world there is usually a reason why something is where it is. If your game has stealth elements, the player may wait to see a pattern emerging in the enemy's path to avoid conflict. If your game is an action based shooter, our player will be likely travel to where they see things come from. Another thing to keep in mind is to know your engine's limitations, especially working within the mobile gamespace, as mobile platforms are much more demanding on the hardware when spawning enemies.

Environment

Pretty art is pretty, but it can't make up for poor design. For artistic people, like me, it can be incredibly easy to fall into the trap of starting to polish up an area before finishing it. After doing preproduction by designing a layout, build your level using BSP additive brushes at first. At this point, the focus in the level is creating an environment that is fun, and has some semblance to the environment that we want the level to take place in. It is important to do whatever we can, to exploit the type of gameplay that we want to occur as well. For example, we could give the player places to hide from enemies and take pot shots, making the player feel smart for outsmarting the enemies.

One of the most important things you can do as a designer is empowering the players as they are not your enemies, they're your best friends, and are ultimately who gives you your pay check, so it's important to respect them. Aside from the actual physical environment, an environment's lighting can be used in many different ways to affect players. Primarily, light draws focus to things and leads players to travel towards it. Darkness and the unknown are uncomfortable areas for players to be in and not lighting areas as much as others adds to the foreboding nature that an area could have. *Monolith's* F.E.A.R. does this quite nicely by turning a regular everyday office into an intense and dangerous place to be in, even though you are fully armed and equipped to handle anything that may come by your way.

Scripting

As important as the placement and spawning of an enemy is, if the enemy doesn't do anything the game will get old quickly. We've created a basic AI for what an enemy could do to enemies, and there are a lot of ways to expand upon it and create unique situations based on what is going on in the game. In large open areas, as long as the player does something resembling intelligence, things seem to go well to which our AI, though limited, can be used to good effect. In general, the tighter the environment, the more you'll want to hand-script the enemy's behavior.

Flanking is a type of behavior in which an enemy is able to come at a target from its sides or behind it, catching it off guard. Flanking in games can be both good and bad. If done well, it can make the player improvise and feel a rush of excitement. If done poorly however, it will make player think AI is cheating, and cause the player to resent the encounter. If you do decide to implement flanking, wait and let the player engage the area before attempting to flank, and make the first shot miss and let the player notice where the shot came from so they can adjust.

Another tool that designers can utilize is the idea of waves in an environment where you spawn different enemies at different times, in order to extend the gameplay and time spent in a certain area. However, each wave should be unique or else the player will get bored easily. *Dungeon Defenders* does this in a good way by incrementing difficulty over time making sure that things don't get boring.

Keep in mind the difficulty of your waves and encounters in general, and modify the elements that you can in order to curve up the difficulty in each encounter, but also give the player a chance to take a breather once in a while to reflect on how powerful he has become.

Playtesting

In my opinion, a game designer is the player's advocate and in that role, their main responsibility is to make a game that your target audience will love. Because of this, playtesters are a game designer's best friend. They are the voice of how a normal person is going to react to your game, and as such it is important that you take what they say seriously. They are the people that are going to find and exploit anything they can get their hands on within your world as well and you will find things you never thought of possible in your game. They are going to suggest changes and it will be your decision whether or not those changes are really worth having or not.

It is also very important that you have people to play your game without your input. Most designers believe that they have covered every possible thing a player can do, but it is almost guaranteed that something has been forgotten. In level design, it is important to see what directions players go in, and whether they are being guided in the correct way.

Summary

We now have all of the pieces that we need to create our game and have learned a lot of things in the process. By using the same principles given in this chapter it is possible to expand and create many different types of enemies and behaviors.

In this short period of time we managed to cover quite a lot of things. We specifically learned the following topics:

◆ What sequences are and how we use them

◆ How to spawn an enemy into our level

◆ What we can do to develop a rudimentary AI system that will shoot at us if we are close to it

◆ How to expand upon that system by adding chasing and retreating behavior

◆ How to create additional enemies using import/export subsequences

◆ How to implement regenerating health using remote events

◆ What prefabs are and how we can and their use them in our project

◆ How to make a door prefab

◆ Things to consider when creating combat scenarios

Now we've learned how to build all of the base elements that we will need to implement our game.

In the next chapter, we will be bringing all of these pieces together to create our full-fledged game by discussing a workflow for creating levels using **Geometry Mode**, how to use modular pieces to create our level quickly, and advice on building levels on your own.

6
Bringing it All Together

In the previous chapter we created a series of sequences and prefabs giving us a solid background for creating different types of assets in our level and giving us some more in depth knowledge of using Kismet as well as an introduction to Prefabs to help us.

In this chapter we are going to expand on the items learned in the previous chapters and "bring it all together" to create our game, Urban Warrior.

In this chapter we will cover the following:

- Setting up our room, learning about adjusting materials to fit your level's needs
- Learn the best way to rapidly prototype levels using reference and placeholder brushes to stand in for art
- Discuss a possible workflow for creating levels using **Geometry Mode**
- Build our level using pieces we've already built, duplicating work we've already done to make building quicker and more streamlined
- Construct different combat scenarios

So with that, let's get started!

Starting a workflow

When I first started using Unreal it took me a lot time to create any type of new level. I would keep placing static meshes to hide areas of geometry that I missed, or adding in blocking volumes in order to make it actually possible to go through some places. One of the key reasons I had problems was that I didn't realize how to create a good workflow, and the key to mapping things in CSG super easily is **Geometry Mode**. Before we take care of that, let's first get our current level ready.

Time for action – starting our level

We are now building our level from scratch using the pieces that we have built in previous chapters. As we already have a basis to draw from let's start our game off. We can start our level as follows:

1. In the Editor, select our **PlayerStart** actor. Move it to the left-hand side of the first door in our level by using Translation Mode.

2. Move the spawn point for our first enemy to be in front of the door using **Translation Mode**. There is a small light blue colored arrow on the actor. The arrow represents the direction in which the actor is facing. With that in mind, rotate the enemy's position in Rotation mode so it is facing away from the hero.

3. Move the **PathNode** such that the second enemy is spawned right in front of the door through which it comes (the second door to the right).

4. Left-click on your current floor of the level and move it down by 32 units, using the grid snap by pressing the [and] keys will decrease and increase the grid snap points until you get there.

5. Change the **World Properties** by selecting **View | World Properties** and set the **Kill Z** to **-64** so we won't die when we hit the floor.

6. Create three walls to encase our hero at his starting point as well as a ceiling above him and floor below him all with a width of **32**. Create the first wall, then by holding *Alt* and dragging the wall in the top viewport, duplicate the original wall to the other side.

7. In front of our door make a duplicate of our floor by moving it 64 units in front, along the axis. Go into **Geometry** mode and hold the *Ctrl + Alt* keys and drag until you select both the vertices on the left-hand side in the top viewport. Drag the floor until it faces the door. Select the two vertices at the top and drag it down until it is in front of the door, and do the same for the bottom. At this point you should have a box in front of your door.

8. Right-click on the side viewport and select **Viewport Type | Front** to place the view into the front mode. Our screen should look like the following screenshot by now.

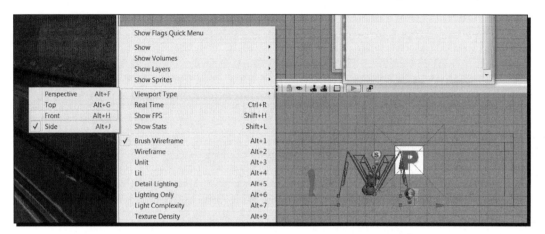

9. At that point in **Geometry** mode select our box and only click on the top right vertex. From there use the translation tool to move it to the left by 64 degrees coming to the same point as the other vertices at the top, as shown in the following image:

10. Build the map by selecting **Build | Build All**. You should see a ramp going into your room that we created.

11. Return the viewport back to its previous position by right-clicking and selecting **Viewport Type | Side**.

12. Press *L* in the center of the room to create a light. Selecting the light, put it in the direct center of the room in the X, Y, and Z axes. Open the **PointLight actor** properties, change its radius to 512, and its **Falloff Exponent** to 16. Inside the **Light Component** set the light color to a light blue and change the brightness to 0.6. Press *Alt + 3* to go into Unlit mode until you are ready to see the game's lighting, but you will have to build every time you change something to see it correctly.

Having a good reference can be key when creating new areas or gameplay. Characters in Unreal are defaulted to 96 units tall and while we can create a box of that size or right-click to get the measuring tape out to adjust, we can just place a mesh in our level to give us an idea of human proportions. Note that this is the character size of Epic Games' characters, but UDK does not limit the size of your characters. If you wish to create your own custom characters you may do so, but it is important that no matter what you remain consistent.

13. Go into the **Content Browser** and scroll your **Packages** column until you can click on **UDK Game**. With that selected type Iron in the search bar while checking the **Skeletal Mesh** option in the **Object Type** field. Left-click on the **IronGuard Skeletal Mesh**. Right-click in our level and place the object on top of the ground in our level. Note that you may have to move the mesh and adjust your grid spacing to get it just right. The following screenshot shows this process.

Having a reference is a great thing, especially if you are trying to recreate a real life building, however note that often at times in games you will have to compensate for different aspects of the world due to the differences in both gameplay and camera work. For example, hallways in games are usually two to three times larger than they would really be especially in games that can be multiplayer, such as *Left 4 Dead*.

14. Left-click on our new actor and open up its properties by clicking *F4*. Type `Hidden` in the search bar and check the **Hidden Game** property.

Since we are in the games ourselves we don't need to see our reference, however if you'd like to keep our new actor in until you're ready then by all means go for it.

15. Select the walls inside of our room by left-clicking on them in the perspective viewport.

16. Select the other walls in the room, taking care to remember that the door has two parts and a top. You can do this by holding *Ctrl* and clicking on each of the elements or right-clicking and selecting **Select Adjacent Walls,** but this option may also select the walls outside of the building as well. Also select the inside of the door, pressing *Alt + W* to hide static meshes to select them, remembering to press *Alt + W* again when finished.

17. Go to the **Content Browser** and pick out a wall material to use. I personally used `M_LT_Walls_BSP_Recycle06b` which is located in the **LT_Walls** package. Once you have left-clicked on the material you wanted to use, right-click on a selected wall in the perspective viewport and select **Add Material : M_LT_Walls_BSP_Recycle06b**. The following image shows the material that has been added to the walls:

Now you may notice that the material may look a bit off in terms of placement and how it doesn't match up; that's okay because that is what we're going to fix next.

18. Press *F5* to enter the **Surface** properties menu. The first and easiest step is to change our alignment so that the brushes will work together so we have a seamless transition between brushes. To do this, find the **Alignment** property, click on the **Box** selection and click on **Apply**. Since our object is in fact shaped similarly to a box, it makes sense that the material can be applied this way, as shown in the following screenshot:

However, I think that the texture is too small for the room I created; this is a simple fix as well. Above the **Alignment** box there is another area of the properties called **Scaling**. Under the **Simple** Option select 2 . 0 and click on the **Apply** button. Now our texture is twice as big as it was before. The **Scaling** box is shown in the following screenshot:

19. Now, we're on the right track, but I want to move the image down and over until I get to just the right place I want the texture to be. Panning the material will do just that. Adjust the **U** and **V** position of the texture by clicking on the buttons until you get the position you want for the material. I personally took the silvery part and made it a baseboard of sorts for my room. This is shown in the following screenshot:

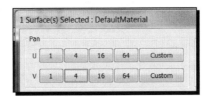

20. Choose a ceiling and floor material for your room. I personally used **Material'LT_Floors.BSP.Materials.M_LT_Floors_BSP_Grate_Pipes** ' for the ceiling and **Material'LT_Floors.BSP.Materials.M_LT_Floors_BSP_Organic05b_ TileBreak'** for the floor.

21. Now that we have our new base room completed, click on the door that we created on the right and delete it, saying **Yes** to the warning generated.

22. Inside the top viewport hold the *Ctrl + Alt* keys and drag until you have the entire room we created selected. Go to **Geometry** mode and right-click on the top right vertices to change the position of our translate tool. Hold *Alt* and drag the item to the right-hand side so that it would be where the previous door would have been. Right-click and select **Transform | Mirror Y Axis** and move the room until it creates a room in front of the one that we previously created. Delete any extra **PathNodes** or **PlayerStart** actors you may have created.

23. Build our game by selecting **Build | Build All** and click on **Close** when finished.

24. Save your project and start your game by clicking on the **Start Mobile Previewer** button on the main toolbar, saying **yes** when it asks you to save the package. The following screenshot shows how our screen would look:

What just happened?

Taking the advice of our former selves our very short scenario is a lot more guided and our world making the game little closer to building our real game. Taking this into consideration we will be able to create a larger environment and complete our sample level.

Geometry mode

We talked about building a simple room earlier in the book, and when we created our doorway in *Chapter 4, Using Kismet and Matinee*, we began to explore **Geometry Mode** and how we can use it. In much the same way we can use it to create gameplay areas quickly and effectively.

Setting up the workflow

You may have noticed a grid of sorts in all the viewports other than the perspective one. We will be using the grid as a guideline in the creation of our levels in much the same way that you could use paper to draw things out, which is something some level designers I know do to get the general feel of an area. In order to build a general area you need to have this planned ahead of time – things such as having a general idea of how you want to place buildings, as well as an idea of how you want to guide the traversal of the player.

As mentioned before, pressing the *[* and *]* keys in the editor will decrease and increase the grid snap points making the level more or less detailed in your brush placement. For the purposes of this book, unless I say differently, I have my grid spacing set to 32. Some people will want to use a smaller area, but I argue that when blocking something out we really only care about the big picture and getting the overall feel of the area. In case your brush is not aligned to the grid you can right-click on the vertices, and it will automatically snap it to the grid. If you notice the brush changing to have an **X** on it, which is alright, but it is advisable to go to the **Brush Properties** and reapply collision to it. This can be extremely useful, especially when working on the things discussed in previous chapters to get it to fit in line with the grid you are now using. Working with the grid is a fundamental way of making sure that you are not getting any holes and/or overlays of your brushes when creating a level. This is another way to make sure that your subtractive brushes will work as you intend them to; however I never use subtractive brushes if I can at all help it.

One thing to note when using **Geometry** mode: you will not see any changes that we make when editing in **Geometry** mode until we build our BSP brushes again.

 In all of the Unreal Tournament games (and **UTDeathmatch** games like we're using), 1 Unreal Unit is equal to 2 centimeters. That means that the 96 Unit character is in fact 6 feet tall! That being said, building things to scale can often seem much smaller than they really are because of the players field of view(FOV)" but it's a nice thing to use as a basis when building from real life.

Some keyboard tips

Holding *Ctrl + Alt* at the same time and dragging will allow you to select all objects that are contained within it. If you are in **Geometry** mode it will allow you to select individual/ overlapping vertices, allowing you to increase or decrease the size of your brushes very easily, which we will be using to create our buildings in the next section.

Another useful tip is if you hold *Ctrl* and drag the left mouse button anywhere in a viewport it will move the brush, actor, and/or vertices that you have selected from any position. This is a good way to move objects that may not be far away or when you don't have to move the screen and don't want to use the widget that is usually used by the object.

If you just left-click on a brush in the perspective viewport it will select the face of the object. While this is fine for putting a material on the brush, on the other viewports it will select the brush for editing. If you hold *Ctrl + Shift* and left-click on your map you will notice that you will now select the brush that you clicked on. However, it can sometimes not pick the brush that you think you're selecting, which is why I primarily use the top and/or side viewport.

Seeing double

Duplicating things that we have already created such as walls or buildings is an effective way of blocking out an environment very quickly. We did this in our previous example by duplicating the room that we created. What we care about most here is creating the best gameplay possible, so we pay less attention to fine details and basically want to just block out an area so we can iterate as quickly as possible. After all, you'd be a lot more willing to get rid of a huge box than a ridiculously detailed office building.

With the brushes we create we can then give the level to your team's environmental artist (or you if you are gifted with 3D modeling knowledge), who will in turn change the BSP brushes into meshes to place in our level to give it the visual flair that we are looking for.

After placing a single brush in our level, you don't really need the builder brush again. Unless you are creating something other than a box you can just duplicate brushes and mould them using the **Geometry** tool to quickly shape out areas, which usually makes it much quicker to build. If you too feel as if you can live without the builder brush, you can press the *B* key to toggle the building brush on and off.

Building our level

With knowledge of how to start a workflow, we can now apply that knowledge by building the rest of our level!

Time for action – building our level

Now that the beginning of our level is completed, let's add simple buildings and shapes that we can fill with the scripting we created earlier! This is done as follows:

1. From the top viewport duplicate one of the walls from the rooms that we made previously by left-clicking on it, holding *Alt* and dragging it down, placing the top end so that the wall covers up the gap between the two doors. In **Geometry** mode grab the two bottom vertices and drag them down to create a square like shape and then in the side viewport drag the vertices up in order to create a building. This is how our screen would look.

2. With that first building created we can build others quite easily. Duplicate it by dragging and create three buildings of different sizes to create a blocking path leading the player towards the left. The following screenshot shows this.

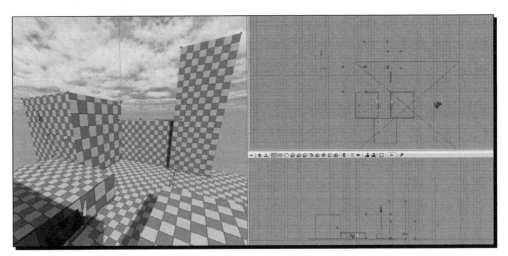

3. Not only can we extend and modify brushes, we can also modify volumes! Extend our current **Lightmass Importance Volume** and floor by selecting both of the objects and dragging them out.

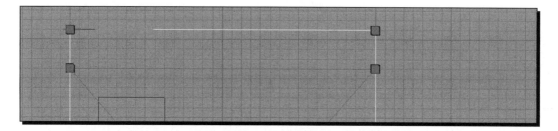

4. Left-click on one of the prefab doors that we have created and create another door, a little distance after the player turns left, making sure to lower the door down so it fits nicely with the ground. We do not want the door to go as far out as the previous version that we created, so select the top six points and drag the door over, adjusting the two at the top afterwards, to create an even door. However, the KActor of the door itself will not change, so right-click on the prefab and select **Convert PrefabInstance into Normal Actors**. From there, you can move the door into its proper spot using the top and side viewports as your guide, building when necessary to help you visualize what the level looks like.

5. Duplicate buildings changing the heights, placing one to the north of the new door that we added and another north of it to open up a little area for the player to explore. This can be seen in the following top viewport screenshot.

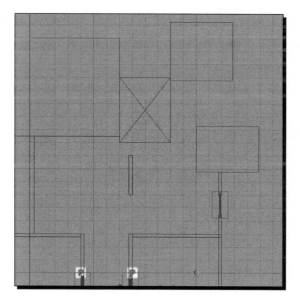

Note that I purposefully made the building in front of the door's holder to show the player that there is a path that can be taken giving the player a sense of choice in the level.

At this point, the player can choose one of two paths, which we will converge into a large area. Create buildings of different sizes and shapes to fill a center courtyard, taking care to make the buildings on the furthest north side the lowest of the bunch as that is where we are going to lead the player.

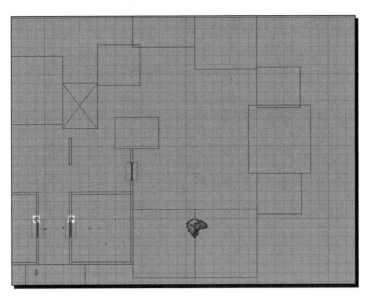

6. In the center of our courtyard place an elevated pedestal by first creating a box around 32 units high. Build the map then left-click on the face of the brush in the perspective viewport. Change to Scaling mode and shrink the top face. If you build the game you will notice that now the brush has slants. Play the game to make sure that you can walk up and down on the pedestal before moving forward.

   Elevated ground will draw the player to this position, plus we will place enemies there later so it's a good way to draw attention to the area.

7. Create ramps leading to the top of the furthest building in much the same way we created ramps for our first room. I personally created a ramp forward, then a straight part and then another ramp for a left turn. This could be done as a fire escape, but we basically want to communicate to the player to go here, as shown in the following screenshot:

8. Expand both your floor and **lightmass Importance Volume** in both the north and east directions by selecting the two vertices at the top and dragging north, then selecting the two vertices on the right-hand side and dragging them east.

9. Create buildings in order to create an enclosed area leading towards a final location which you will leave open and will be four grid squares wide at a grid snap of 128.

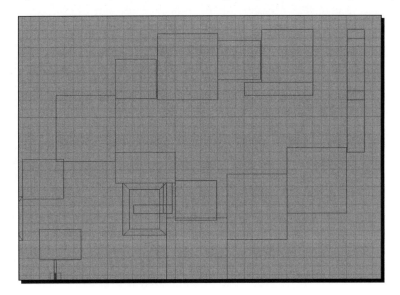

10. At the center of the open space that you have created place the `StaticMesh'ASC_Floor2.SM.Mesh.S_ASC_Floor2_SM_Stairs_Simple_01'`. To each of its sides create a ramp shape to cover up its sides.

11. Above the two ramps that you have created create two vertically large pillars. On the top of the pillar place another brush that is slanted.

12. Create a ceiling and a floor to the entrance we've created.

13. Take the two long pillars that we created and duplicate them within the temple.

14. Past the second pillar create a secondary flight of stairs and a floor ahead for its elevated path.

15. In front of the floor place a single wall behind it and walls on the sides of the temple.

16. In front of the second flight of stairs place a `StaticMesh'NR_Deco.SM.Mesh.S_NR_Deco_SM_FountainTop03'` and above it `ParticleSystem'Castle_Assets.FX.P_FX_Fire_SubUV_01'` and above that a spot light (by pressing *L* and clicking inside the viewport where you want it to be placed) with a radius of `1024`, a `.3` brightness, and a dark red color. Inside the **lightmass** settings change the light source to `32` and duplicate the items to the other side of the stairs as well.

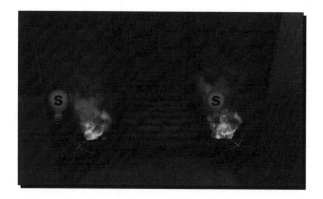

17. Now do a quick texture pass by using `Material'LT_Floors.BSP.Materials.M_LT_Floors_BSP_Dark_TileBreak_02'` for the walls and `Material'LT_Floors.BSP.Materials.M_LT_Floors_BSP_Organic05b_TileBreak'` for the floor and ceiling of our temple. Select all of the materials and give it a simple scaling of `4.0`.

18. Select the **Dominant Directional Light** actor and change its light color to dark blue.

19. Outside the player's path but in their view, place some `StaticMesh'LT_Mech.SM.Mesh.S_LT_Mech_SM_CityNoRing01'` actors to create scenery for our level. Note that this mesh was created for the PC multiplayer title Unreal Tournament 3 and has in no way been optimized for a mobile game. That being said, don't place more than four in the level or else the game will really start to slow down when we test it. The following screenshot is what the finished level will look like:

What just happened?

Our level now has a clear beginning, middle, and end. The goals for the player to go to as well as some backdrop and lighting effects are visible. Now all we need to do is add our interactive elements and we will have our game completed!

Have a go hero – powerups and weapon pickups

One of the tools that level designers have is the ability to reward players for traveling certain ways. Promoting exploration and giving players reason to go out will make your level much more interesting. Inside the **Actor** classes tab there is a class called **UTPickupFactory** with both **Health** and **Weapon** pickups. Try to place some goodies in your newly created level. I personally put a rocket launcher in the area leading up to the temple.

Combat scenarios

As we are in fact making a third person shooter, it makes sense that we would want to have different combat scenarios in our game. After completing our level's layout we will now add the things that will make our level come alive! We went over the creation of enemies as well as advice on combat scenarios in the previous chapter, so now we will be acting upon these lessons to create our own game.

Time for action – first combat scenario

We will be using trigger volumes to spawn enemies and have them interact in your environment. This can be done as follows:

1. In the Editor, duplicate the top part of the door that goes into the second area and move it so that its front is joined with the building we created with the split. Right-click on the actor and select **Convert | Convert to Volume | Trigger Volume**. After this go to the side viewport and adjust the bottom vertices so they hit the floor. Hint: Pressing *Alt + W* will make the static meshes that we've placed previously disappear. The following screenshot shows this:

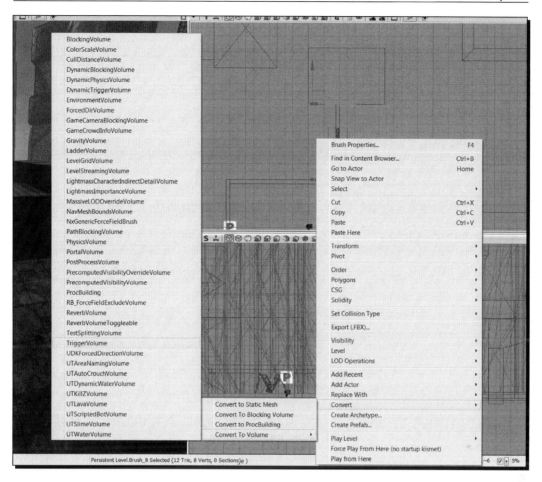

2. Duplicate the trigger volume that we have just created and place it directly above where this one is. This way, no matter which way the player chooses to go something will happen.

3. We will place two path nodes behind each of the two routes we have created as well as two path nodes in the middle. What we are going to do is spawn two enemies when the player hits one of these triggers, and the two enemies will travel along the path the player first chose, as shown in the following screenshot:

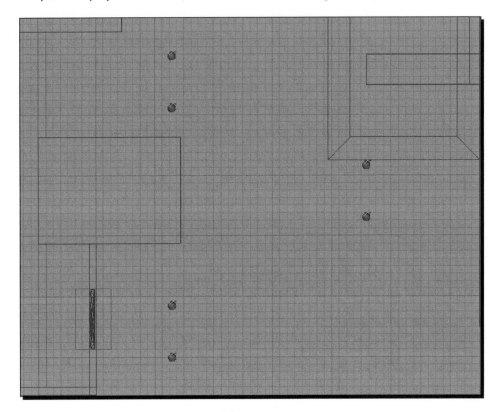

Left-click on the trigger volume at the top that we created and open Kismet. Create a **TriggerVolume Touch** event by choosing **New Event using TriggerVolume_5 | Touch** from the menu that pops up.

4. Left-click on the trigger volume that we created at the bottom and open Kismet. Create a **TriggerVolume Touch** event beneath the one that we just created by choosing **New Event using TriggerVolume_6 | Touch** from the menu that pops up.

5. Create a **Toggle** action by right-clicking and selecting **New Action | Toggle | Toggle**. Connect the **Event** link to the top of the **TriggerVolume_5 Touch** action. Connect the **Out** output of the **TriggerVolume_6 Touch** action to the **Turn Off** input of this Toggle action.

6. Create another toggle action to turn the other action off if this one is called. The following screenshot shows what we've done so far:

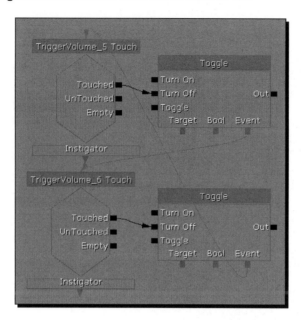

7. For each of the two paths, create two set **Object** actions by selecting **New Action | Set Variable | Object**. Under the **Value** variable link place the two top path nodes we created to the top trigger and the bottom two to the other. Don't worry about the target yet, we will come to that in a later step.

8. Copy and paste two copies of the **EnemyAI** subsequence that we created earlier right next to each other. Connect the **Out** of both the second **Set Object** variable outputs to the **In** of the first **EnemyAI** object and the **Spawned** output of the first connects to the **In** of the second. Create an Object variable underneath the **Spawned** link for each node and make the two path nodes we placed out of player sight as the spawn points for both objects.

9. Create a **Move To Actor** action by right-clicking and selecting **New Action | AI | Move To Actor**. Underneath the **Target** variable link connect the first spawned object that we created. Under **Destination** create an **Object** variable and connect it. Connect the **Spawned** output from the **EnemyAI** action to the **In** input on the **Move To Actor** action. Also, in the **Set variable** actions that we discussed in Step 5 connect the **Target** variable link for the first object in each row to this object.

10. Now create a second **Move to Actor** action using the **Spawned** variable link of the second **EnemyAI** as the **Target** and create a new **Object** variable under the **Destination** link, which you will set as the **Target** of the second **Set Object** in each path.

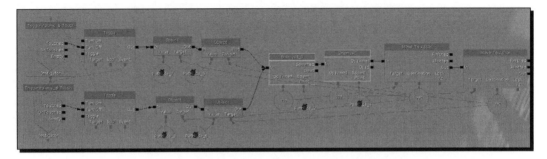

At some point during this tutorial you may see a problem and/or an error in your project saying something along the lines of **SeqAct_ActorFactory_0 has no spawn points!** In that case, go into Kismet where that problem node is, double click on it to select it in the editor and double-click on the **Enemy_AI Sequence** it contains. At the **Actor Factory** action click on the plus icon to add a new item to the spawn point list and if it isn't filled already click on the arrow pointing left in order to fill the value with the object we have selected. Exit the subsequence and hook up the items again that were attached to it. When you run your game next it should start working again.

11. Build our game by selecting **Build | Build All** and click **Close** when finished.

12. Save your project and start your game by clicking on the **Start Mobile Previewer** button on the main toolbar. The game's preview should look like the following screenshot:

What just happened?

With only a little bit of effort we have easily created a second combat encounter in the game that adjusts itself based on player actions.

Have a go hero – creating your own combat encounter

The next section I am going to leave as a blank area for you to create some kind of combat encounter of your own. You can place pieces of cover, or alternate weapons. Try to think of something that will really make someone say, "Wow!" when they see it.

Time for action – end of level

We will be using trigger volumes to spawn enemies and have them interact in your environment.

1. Place a trigger volume in front of the temple that we created earlier. At the back of the temple as well as behind the second pillar place path nodes on both sides, away from the player's line of sight. This is shown by the top viewport screenshot:

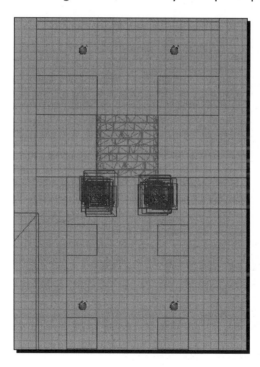

This is how it will look in the game.

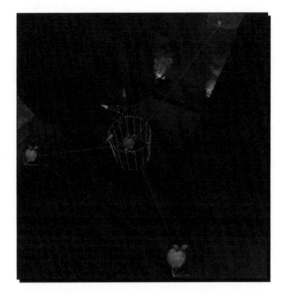

Press the *P* button to see the paths that have been created by your path nodes. If you do not see any lines in-between the two sets of nodes you may have to place one or two extra nodes to make sure the enemies' paths are laid out correctly.

2.   Left-click on our trigger volume and create a **Trigger Volume Touch** event in Kismet.

3.   Copy and paste the two **EnemyAI** and **Move to Actor** actions from the previous example and hook it up to the **Trigger Volume Event**.

4.   Delete the spawn point links and replace them with the two nodes at the top of the temple. Delete the **Destination** links in the **Move to Actor** events and have them travel to the path nodes in the front.

5.   Duplicate your trigger volume and put it at the top of the temple's hill. Create a Touch event with a **Console Command** event with **quit** at the prompt.

6.   Build our game by selecting **Build | Build All** and click on **Close** when finished.

7.   Save your project and start your game by clicking on the **Start Mobile Previewer** button on the main toolbar.

What just happened?

We created a new combat scenario in which the enemies run into cover leaving themselves vulnerable while letting the player know that they're there. We also created an end point to the level which allows us to complete the game. The following screenshot show this:

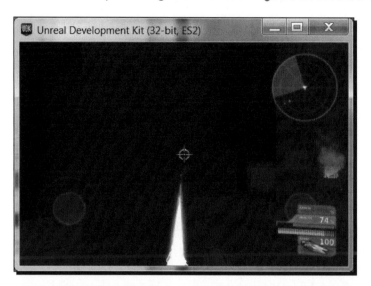

Pop quiz

1. What are some of the problems with creating a level without using grid snaps?

    a. Holes in our geometry.

    b. Overlapping brushes.

    c. Ensuring subtractive brushes work correctly.

    d. All of the above.

2. What keys do you use in order to increase or decrease grid snaps?

    a. + and −.

    b. Left and right arrow keys.

    c. [and].

    d. (and).

3. Is it possible to have an event with a Max Trigger Count of 0 (Can be triggered as many times as you'd like) to no longer be triggered? If possible, how would I do that?

    a. False, we can't toggle an Event on and off.

    b. False, the Max Trigger Count has to be positive.

    c. True, we can toggle an Event on and off.

    d. True, it's done automatically.

Summary

We have now reached the end of our game development section of the book. There is plenty of room now for you to make your project your own, add new levels, and explore the different aspects of the Unreal Engine; we have built the foundation of a truly awesome game.

In this short period of time we've managed to cover quite a lot of things.
We've specifically learned:

♦ How to set up our room learning about adjusting materials to fit your level's needs

♦ The best way to rapidly prototype out levels using reference and placeholder brushes to stand in for art

♦ A possible workflow for creating levels using **Geometry** mode

♦ How to build our level using pieces we've already built duplicating work we've already done to make building quicker and more streamlined

♦ The implementation of different combat scenarios

Now that we've learned how to build the level and created all of the gameplay sections, in the next chapter I will be showing you how to add a main menu as well as play sounds, integrate custom content into your game, discuss optimizing, and debug your iOS game project to polish it as much as we can before we put it up on the App Store!

7

Advanced Content Creation for Urban Warrior

With our game level finished from the previous chapter, we now have a level that has been playtested and we know that it is quite fun. Now that we have a great base to build on we can create our own content for our game to customize it and make the game really your own.

In this chapter we shall discuss the following:

- ◆ Creating a main menu for our game with input
- ◆ Adding audio on mobile UDK for our game
- ◆ Importing custom textures to our game
- ◆ Creating materials for both PC and iOS to use
- ◆ Adding static meshes on mobile UDK for our game
- ◆ Some tips for optimization and debugging on the iOS

The assets that I will be bringing into the game in this level will be available on the Packt Publishing website, but with the information contained in this chapter it should be fairly easy to create assets of your own that you can bring into the game. With that being said, let's begin!

Downloading the example code

You can download the example code files for all Packt books you have purchased from your account at `http://www.packtpub.com`. If you purchased this book elsewhere, you can visit `http://www.packtpub.com/support` and register to have the files e-mailed directly to you.

Main menu environment creation

As nice as dropping right in the action of a game is, most games have a menu of some sort. This will also be a nice way of showing you how we can use aspects that we have already covered before doing something different.

Time for action – building main menu backdrop

Sure, most menus in a game look like they're something special, but in reality they are just a new level. To build the main menu backdrop perform the following steps:

1. First, let's open up the map that we previously used in *Chapter 3, Taking It to the Next Level; Enriching with Content*. Select the skydome and the two directional lights we created and copy them by pressing *Ctrl+C*, this is shown in the following screenshot:

2. Create a new level by selecting **File | New...** and select the **Blank Map** template. Paste the objects into your level.

3. Right-click on the **Cube** icon on the left-hand side toolbar directly underneath the **Brushes** text. In the settings for the builder brush check the **Hollow** option. This will create a hollow cube. Click on the **Build** button and then add the geometry to our level by clicking on the **CSG_Add** option that we used in *Chapter 2, Beginning Urban Warrior; A First Person Shooter* or by using *Ctrl+A*.

4. Move the camera inside of the box and create a **Player Start** actor by right-clicking and selecting **New Actor | New Player Start**. If the object has a red **X** on it move the object until it has plenty of space on all sides in order to spawn the player there:

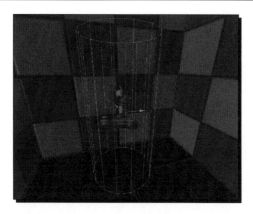

5. Access the **WorldInfo Properties** by going to the top menu and selecting **View | World Properties**. In the **Game Type** section set the **Default Game Type** and **Game Type** for PIE to **MobileMenuGame**.

6. By either copying and pasting from the actual game level or finding `StaticMesh'LT_Mech.SM.Mesh.S_LT_Mech_SM_CityNoRing01` inside the Content Borwser, place two of the objects into your game world in such a way that they have buildings in all angles.

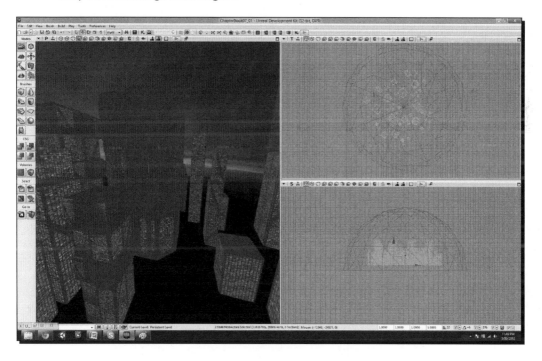

7. Go to the **Actor Classes** tab by selecting **View | Browser Windows | Actor Classes**. Select the **CameraActor** found in **Common | CameraActor** and exit the building. Create a camera by right-clicking and selecting **Add Camera Actor Here**. Position the camera in the middle of your area, tilted slightly to the sky. In particular you want to make sure that you cannot see the hollow box we created earlier. If it's easier for you to move it out of the way, feel free to do that.

8. Press *F4* in order to access the Camera Actor's properties. In the **Movement** section change the **Physics** property to **PHYS_Rotating**. Select the **Yaw** section of the **Rotation Rate** and set it to 20. This special type of physics will move the actor along the rotation rate but will not be able to do anything else. This would be great for our main menu as we just want a nice background effect to show up. This is how the Camera Actor's property window will look:

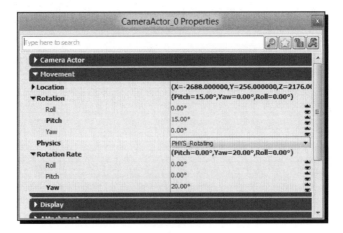

9. With our level created and our **CameraActor** selected let's go into Kismet. Create a **Level Loaded Event (New Event | Level Loaded)**. To its right-hand side create a new Matinee by right-clicking and selecting **New Matinee**. Connect the **Loaded** and **Visible** output of the **Level Loaded** event to the **Play** action of the **Matinee** and double-click on the **Matinee** to enter the Matinee editor.

10. Create a camera track with the name `Turning Camera` by right-clicking and selecting **Add New Camera Group**. Then create a new **Director Group** by right-clicking and selecting **Add New Director Group**. Add a **Keyframe** at the beginning of the Matinee sequence and select **Turning Camera** at the **Cut To Group** option that comes up. Close the Matinee editor.

11. Back in Kismet select the Matinee object and make sure that the **Looping** option is checked. Exit Kismet.

12. Create a **Lightmass Importance Volume** to cover the area around the player including the buildings. Also make sure that the lights are not inside any of the buildings, move them if you need to.

13. Build our game by selecting **Build | Build All** and clicking on **Close** when finished.

14. Save your project and start your game by clicking on the **Start Mobile Previewer** button. This is how your screen should look:

What just happened?

We now see a nice cityscape as our camera pans around at a constant rate. This will be a nice looking background for our title screen, and with this as a basis we can build our main menu.

Importing textures

A mobile graphics hardware works with different formats and handles textures differently than a normal PC graphics hardware. By taking the necessary precautions and creating textures accordingly, many obstacles can be avoided. Now, I'm by no means an art expert but I'll briefly go over some things that you should abide by if you do decide to do your own textures for iOS.

When creating your own textures it is important to make the size of the image in powers of two such as 256, 512, 1024, and 2048. Computers process data in "chunks" for purposes of efficiency. For game content creation, on devices mobile especially, if a texture is not in a power of two Unreal will waste resources both in terms of time and processing power in order fix the problem. In effect the essence of the power of two rule is optimization, being as efficient and as "lite" as possible while providing the user an appropriate visual experience. When working with iOS, hardware textures can have a size of up to 2048 by 2048 but use them sparingly. This is particularly important in the case of games targeting lower end devices (such as iPhone 3GS, iPad 1, and iPod touch 4th generation) that only have 256 MB of RAM.

The following texture formats are supported: `.bmp`, `.pcx`, `.png`, `.tga`, `.float` and `.psd`.

Time for action – finishing the main menu

That being said, let's import our first texture into the game:

1. Open up the **Content Browser** by either selecting its icon or going to the **View** menu and selecting **View | Browser Windows | Content Browser**. Click on the **Import** button in the menu at the bottom of the window. Find the image that you would like to bring into the game and select **Open**:

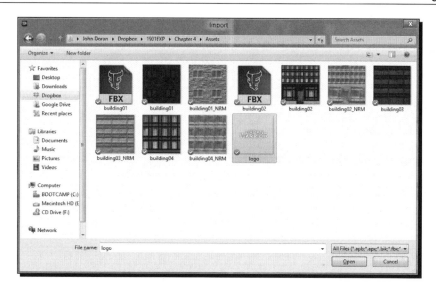

2. There will be an import dialog that will come up. In the **Packages** section type the name `UW-MainMenuPKG` and confirm that `logo` is in the **Name** section. You should be brought back to the **Content Browser** where you will see our new package with one new file:

3. Underneath the **New Packages** option in the **Packages** section on the left-hand side toolbar, right-click on the package that we just created and select **Save** to save the package as a file. It is important to save things often to make sure you don't lose your work:

Close the **Content Browser** and go back into Kismet. Create a **Draw Image event** by right-clicking and selecting **New Event | HUD | Draw Image**. In the properties for it select the **Display Color** as white. In the **Display Location** section set the **X** value to .25. Set the **XL** and **YL** to 0.5 and **UL** and **VL** to 512. It is important to note that this Kismet event doesn't give you the option to do proper scaling for aspect ratio differences so more complex logos may be squished, so play with the values until you find what works for you. Check the **Is Active** checkbox and change the **Authorized Global Scale** to 1.0. Go to the **Content Browser** and left-click on our logo image. In the **Draw Image** properties click on the green arrow next to the **Display Texture** option in order to set our logo image in the world. Place a Player 0 variable underneath the Target by right clicking and selecting **New Variable | Player | Player**. Inside the **Player** variable uncheck the **All Players** checkbox in its properties. A few of the changes we made are seen in the following screenshot:

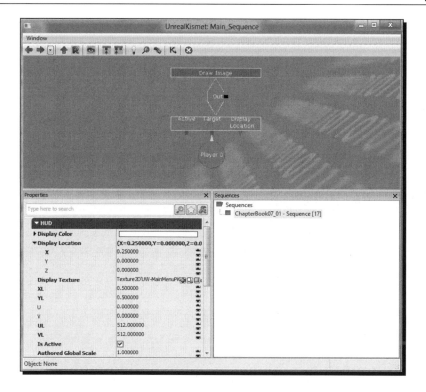

4. Save your project and start your game by clicking on the **Start Mobile Previewer** button. This is how the preview would look:

We now have a title that follows us when we start the game, but as of right now nothing happens and there's no way to start the game properly. What we're going to do next is place some text that says **"Tap anywhere to begin"** in the middle of the screen and then create a button which when tapped will open our main game level. Knowing what we plan on doing, let's do that now!

5. Open up the **Content Browser** by going to the **View** menu and selecting **View | Browser Windows | Content Browser**. In the **Object Type** section change the tab from **Favorites** to **All Types** and check **Fonts**. In the search bar type 36 and left-click on the font on the bottom which specifically is Font'UI_Fonts.Fonts.UI_ Fonts_Positec36'. With it selected, open up Kismet.

6. Go back to Kismet and create a **Show Text** event by right-clicking next to the **Draw Image** event and selecting **New Event | HUD | Draw Text**. In the **Properties** section click on the green arrow next to **Display Font** to set the font we are going to use. Change the **Display Color** to white. On the **Display Location** put **X** as `.5`, **Y** as `.75` to be directly below our image and **Z** to `0`. In the **Display Text** section type `Tap anywhere to begin!`. Change the **Text Draw Method** to **DRAW_CenterText** and check the **Is Active** checkbox . Change the **Authorized Global Scale** to `1.0`. Underneath the **Target** place a Player 0 variable by right-clicking and selecting **New Variable | Player | Player** and uncheck the **All Players** checkbox in its properties. A few of the changes we made are seen in the following screenshot:

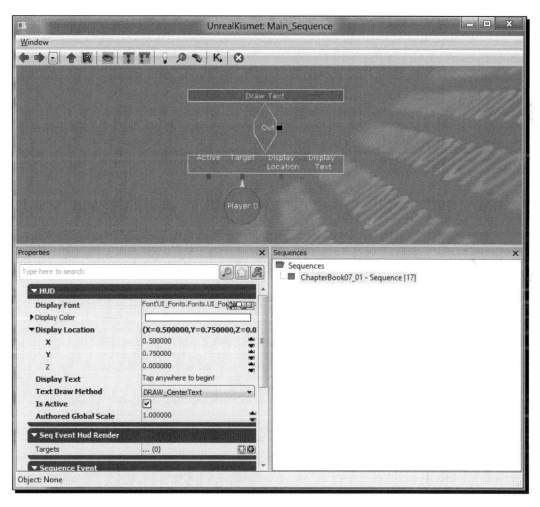

7. Create a bool variable underneath the **Active** section on the **Draw Text Event** by right-clicking on the square under the word and selecting **Create New Bool Variable**. Move the Matinee Sequence we just created in the **Level Loaded** event by selecting it and its associated object, and hold the *Ctrl* key to move it by dragging your left mouse button. To the right of the **Level Loaded** event create a new **Toggle** action by right-clicking and selecting **New Action | Toggle | Toggle**. Connect the **Loaded and Visible** output to the **Toggle** input of **Toggle**. Connect the **Bool** input of **Toggle** to the bool on our **Draw Text** action. Connect the **Out** from the **Toggle** event to the **Toggle** input of it and right click on the **Out** output and click on **Set Activate Delay** and give it a value of 0.1 as shown in the following screenshot:

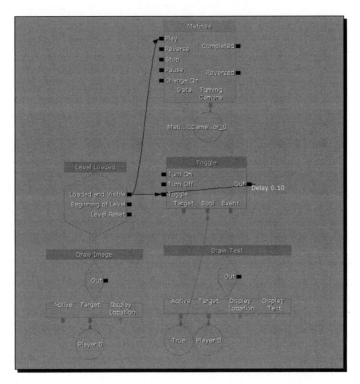

8. Now that we have the blinking text saying to hit the button, how about we create a button to respond to the players touch? Remove the connection between the **Loaded and Visible** output of the **Level Loaded** event and the **Toggle** input of the **Toggle** event, move it over to the right and create an **Add Input Zone** action by right-clicking and selecting **New Action | Mobile | Add Input Zone**. Set the **Zone Name** to StartGame. Click on the little blue triangle next to the **New Zone** to create a new **MobileInputZone**. Inside the **Zone** you just created, in the **Bounds** section set the **Authored Global Scale** to 1.0 and the **Size X** and **Size Y** to 1.0 and check **Relative Size X** and **Relative Size Y** checkboxes, as shown in the following screenshot:

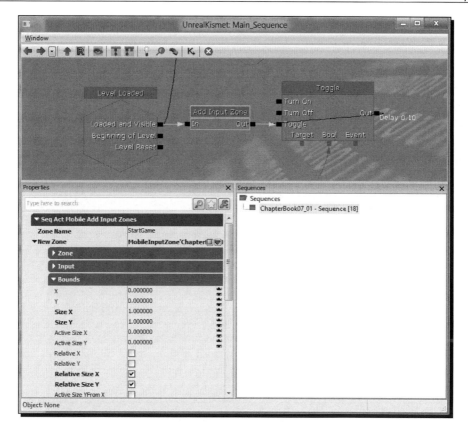

Now that we have a button created (it's invisible so you can't see it, but I assure you it's there) we should work on creating some sort of interaction when it happens.

9. Create a **Mobile Button Access** event by right-clicking and selecting **New Event | Input | Mobile Button Access**. Inside the properties under **Seq Event Mobile Zone Base** in the **Target Zone Name** put the zone we created earlier, StartGame. In the **Sequence Event** section change the **Re Trigger Delay** to 1.0. In the **Sequence Object** properties under **Obj Comment** type Pressed and then the check **Output Obj Comment To Screen** checkbox.

    Inside the Unreal Editor it is not possible to open up other levels, however it will work in the actual game. This is just to verify that the button does indeed work for us.

10. Create a **Console Command** action by right-clicking and selecting **New Action | Misc | Console Command**. In the **Commands** section under **[0]** type `open levelname` where `levelname` is the name of the level you want to load. Create a **Player 0** variable underneath the **Target** of the **Console Command**. Remember that when you are ready to publish the game, remove the comments that you created.

11. Save your project and start your game by clicking on the **Start Mobile Previewer** button. The preview will look like the following screenshot:

What just happened?

With that, we have created a main menu such that when we tap the screen will go into our game level creating a professional looking start to our game.

Adding sounds

Something that many people take for granted, sound, can have a massive effect on people when they are playing your game. To give you a taste of how simple it is to add sounds to your game let's add one when we start the game.

However, just because it is easy to add sounds to our game, playing sounds on iOS devices is quite hard to do—it takes a lot of computing as an iOS device is only able to play one at a time; this is because sounds that are played are uncompressed. This is unlike music that you listen to on your computer (unless you are an audiophile) which is compressed in a format like MP3 which uses a compression algorithm to keep the size of files small. However, having uncompressed sounds makes the files a lot larger. Initializing multiple sounds in the same frame can cause a lot of performance problems. It is a good idea to not play multiple sounds at once if you can help it. This being said, you're going to want to make them as small as possible. Using 22 kHz sounds over 44 kHz sounds on iOS is an easy way to gain a lot of performance that would otherwise be going into processing the sound files. Given that the typical use case of an iOS device is either going to be over the bad speaker or bad headphones included with the device, you can gain a lot of performance for minimal sound difference.

Time for action – playing a sound effect

We want the player to know that we have understood him/her tapping to start the game. Let's play a sound to show him/her we know. We can do this as follows:

1. Open up the **Content Browser** by either selecting its icon or going to the **View** menu and selecting **View | Browser Windows | Content Browser** . Click on the **Import** button in the menu at the bottom of the window. Find the sound that you would like to bring into the game and select **Open**. In the window that pops up set the package with the same name that you just created and open up the tab in the Options menu and check **Auto Create Cue** then click on **OK,** saying yes if it asks you to import the entire package.

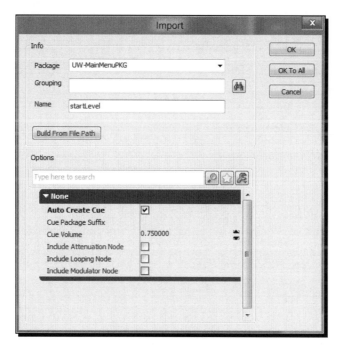

2. Right-click on the package name on the left-hand side of the **Content Browser** and save our package by selecting **Save** on the menu. Left-click on the **Sound Cue** object and exit into Kismet.

3. Inside Kismet disconnect the **Console Command** action that we created previously by holding down *Alt* and clicking on the line connecting it from the **Mobile Button Access** event and move it to the right by holding *Ctrl* and dragging. In the space available create a **Play Sound** action by right-clicking and selecting **New Action | Sound | Play Sound**. In the **Play Sound** action's properties click on the green arrow in the **Play Sound** property to set it to the sound we created. Connect the **Input Pressed** output from the **Mobile Button Access** event to the **Play** on the **Play Sound** action and the **Finished** from the **Play Sound** action to the **Console Command** event. Your screen should look like the following screenshot:

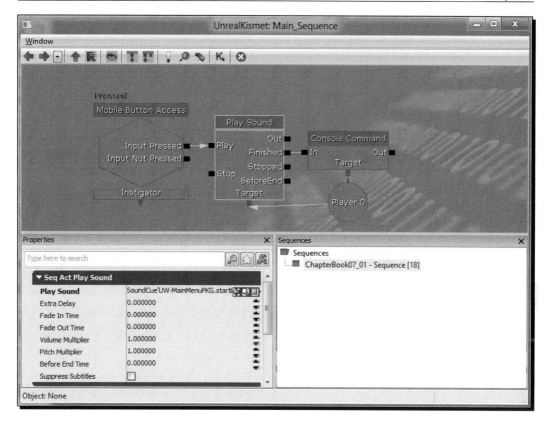

4. Save your project and start your game by clicking on the **Start Mobile Previewer** button.

What just happened?

And now our menu creates a sound whenever we tap the screen!

Customizing sounds

Note that the way that I'm doing sound right now doesn't take into account the sound's position in space. This doesn't matter since the sound is going to be playing directly at the player, but if you wanted to, you can edit the **SoundCue** by right-clicking on it in the **Content Browser** and selecting **Edit Using SoundCue Editor**.

The SoundCue Editor is very similar to Kismet other than the fact that the only event called is when it is played which is shown by an image of a Speaker. The **attenuation** feature can be applied to events in order to put a given sound into world space instead of it always being the same. However, this can only work if the sound is a mono sound.

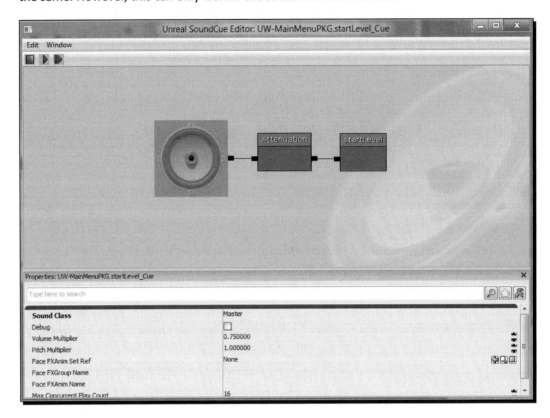

Once this is set it is possible to drag-and-drop a SoundCue inside a level, into the game world. So if you would like to add sound effects in your level that way you are welcome to try this and when you go around your level the sound will become louder and shift location based on where you are in the game world. There are plenty of other features to look at here, such as randomizers, but we'll only be playing a simple sound here. Play around with it in your own time or look at the Sound Cues that Epic provides with UDK to see the possible things you can do, such as adding modulation and variation to sounds, just like the gun shots sound different depending on your location in the game world, when you fire them. Have fun with it!

Adding music

Similar to sound, music is done slightly differently on iOS than they are done for the PC. Since mobiles are usually media players they have hardware that specifically works with playing music efficiently, but the mobile platform is also limited in what it can do. Let's first add some music to our level.

Time for action – adding a background music track

Now, mobile devices have dedicated sound hardware for compressed sounds. iOS devices can play back one compressed stream at a time with little to no cost, so it will be our job to create music that works well in that regard. However, MP3 files do not work in the PC version of Unreal in either the editor or main game so I will be showing you how to add music in the Editor as well. We can do this as follows:

1. Go to Windows Explorer and open your `UDKGame\Build\iPhone\Resources\Music` folder. This is the folder that you need to place any MP3 file that you want to play within your game. For the sake of this we will be using a file already included with UDK, but feel free to put in any MP3 file that you like and whenever I say `Jazz_Menu_01`, type the name of your file. The music folder would look like the following screenshot:

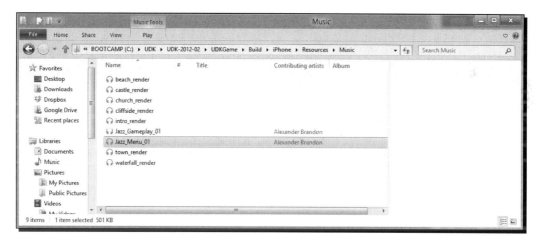

2. Open the **Content Browser** by either selecting its icon or going to the **View** menu and selecting **View | Browser Windows | Content Browser**. Inside the **Content Browser** change the **Object Type** to **Sound Cues** and type music in the textbox at the top of the window. Left-click on the first item which is SoundCue'A_Music_ GoDown.MusicSegments.A_Music_GoDown_Ambient01Cue' and exit into Kismet. The following screenshot shows this:

Note that this file will not be used in the game when it goes on an iOS device, but will let you know that for sure that sound is playing. If you had your own music file you could export it with Audacity (http://audacity. sourceforge.net/) and import it in much the same way that you would for sound effects, but that is a good exercise to do on your own.

3. In Kismet remove the connection between the **Loaded and Visible** output on the **Level Loaded** event and the **In** section of the **Add Input Zone** action. Move the **Level Loaded** action to the left by holding *Ctrl* and dragging. In the space created right-click and create a **Play Music Track** action by right-clicking and selecting **New Action | Sound | Play Music Track**. Connect the **Loaded and Visible** output from the **Level Loaded** event into the **In** of the **Play Music Track** and the **Out** from the **Play Music Track** action into the **In** of the **Add Input Zone** action. Inside the properties for the **Play Music Track** action extend the **Seq Act Play Music Track** section. Click on the green arrow next to the **Sound Cue** to set the PC version of music to play, and then at the bottom of the screen you will see **MP3Filename** where you will put Jazz_ Menu_01.

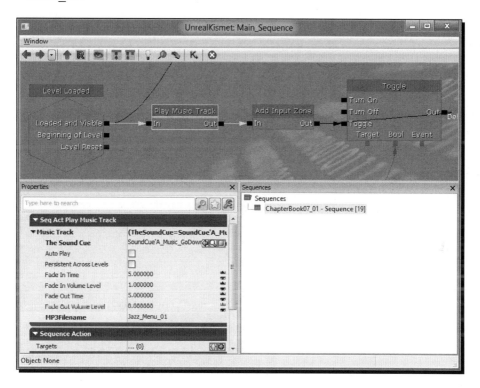

4. Save your project and start your game by clicking on the **Start Mobile Previewer** button.

What just happened?

With that, we have created a main menu that when tapped will go into our game level creating a professional looking start to our game.

Custom materials

Materials are what the Unreal Engine uses in order to put images onto brushes or 3D models that we've created; now, we'll get to putting in custom models in a minute, but first we need to get materials in and for those that don't know how to use a 3D modeling program this will be the extent of what they can do, without learning another program. There are also some stunning professional-quality maps made only using Materials and BSPs and minimal meshes such as the *Hardcore Oldskool Low-Poly Map Pack* at `http://holp.beyondunreal.com/index.html`, so you don't have to learn one if you don't want to, but it helps.

Time for action – customizing brushes

The level that we created in the previous chapter does indeed look good, but it would be even better to put actual buildings into the level, so let's try to make the brushes more building-like by adding some custom Materials to them!

1. Open up the **Content Browser** by either selecting its icon or going to the **View** menu and selecting **View | Browser Windows | Content Browser**. Click on the **Import** button in the menu at the bottom of the window. Select both the files `building03` and `building03_NRM` by clicking on one, holding down the *Ctrl* key and selecting the other. With these selected click on **Open**. This is how your screen would look:

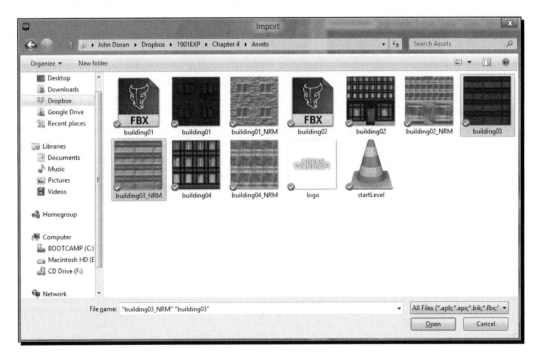

2. There will be an import dialog that will come up. In the **Package** section type the name UW-GamePKG and confirm that building03 is in the **Name** section. Inside the **Options** section check the box for **Create Material** and click on **OK** and then for the building03_NRM file uncheck the **Create Material** option and click on **OK**. You should be brought back to the **Content Browser** where you will see our new package with three new files, as shown in the following screenshot:

3. Double-click on the building03_Mat material in order to enter the **Material Editor**. Now the **Material Editor** may look scary at first, but just like the Sound Editor it is amazingly similar to Kismet when you look at it. Click on the **Texture Sample** with the texture that we imported and drag it to the right-hand side of the **Diffuse** option by holding *Ctrl* and dragging.

4. Go to the **Content Browser** and select the `building03_NRM` texture by left-clicking it and going back into the **Material Editor**. Hold down the *T* key and left-click on the screen near the **Normal** section of the **PreviewMaterial_0** area, you should see a new Texture Sample show up. You also select the Texture Sample from the menu on the right-hand side and drag-and-drop it in from the **Material Expressions** area. Connect the **Normal** option from the **PreviewMaterial_0** to the black connector of the new **Texture Sample**.

You will notice that our Material now looks like it has depth to it. That is because a normal map is a technique used for faking the lighting of bumps and dents. It is used to add details without using more polygons and what you see now is how it would look if you played your game on PC. When playing the game on iOS, UDK will attempt to bake it into the lightmap used by the level using the PC materials normal map, while the advanced effects use the normal map slot under the **Mobile** section of the material editor.

Again, there are a lot of other options that you can use on the PC version of UDK that you cannot use on the iOS. However, there is a very good guide for those who want to create their own textures on the different things you can do on UDN at `http://udn.epicgames.com/Three/MobileMaterialReference.html`.

5. Deselect the **Texture Sample** and you should see the **Properties** for the Material at the bottom of the screen. Open up the **Mobile** section by click on the green arrow beside **Mobile Normal Texture** in order to load our normal map into the game. Go into the **Content Browser** and select our diffuse texture and then click the green arrow for **Mobile Base Texture**. The **Material Editor** window will look like the following screenshot:

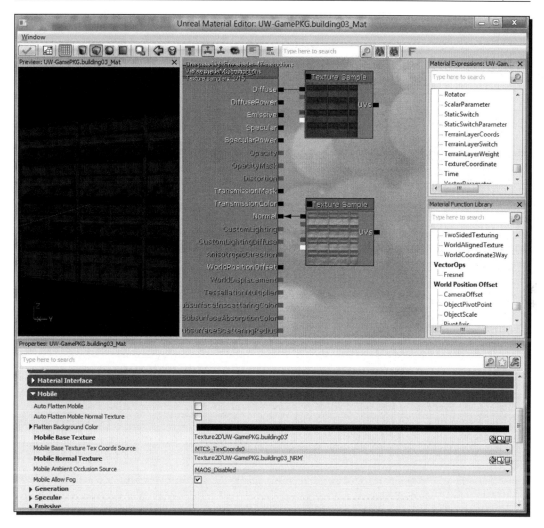

6. In the menu click on the green checkmark at the top in order to save the changes that you've made and close the **Material Editor**. Save the package you've created by right-clicking on the package and selecting **Save** from the menu and saving the package in a location on your computer.

7. Repeat steps 1 to 6 for the other materials in the folder as we will be using them later.

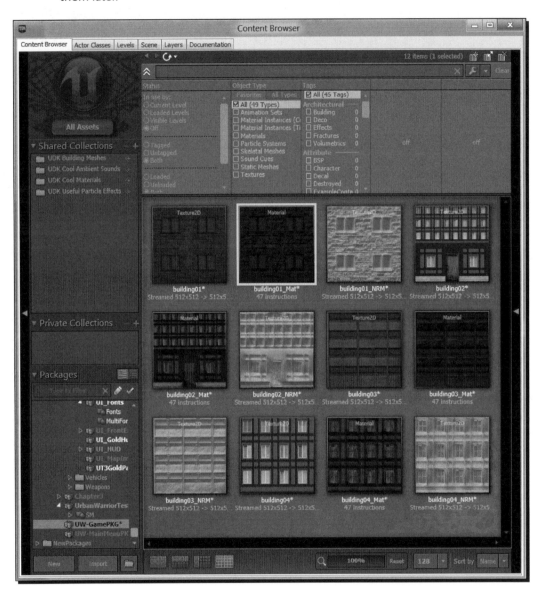

8. Open up the game level that we created in the previous chapter. Find a large brush that you created for a building before, left-click to select one of the surfaces then right-click and select **Select Surfaces | Matching Brush**. Go to the **Content Browser** and select `building01_Mat` by left-clicking on it. At the brush right-click and select **Apply Material : building01_Mat**. You may click on the **Unlit** button on the perspective toolbar or press *Alt+3* to help you see what's going on. When you are finished you can press *Alt+4* to go back to **Lit** mode.

9. We can start to see how the building could work out using this material, but each side seems to be doing its own thing in the different coordinates, thankfully we can easily fix this problem.

10. Open up the **Surface Properties** menu by either pressing *F5* or going to **View | Surface Properties** and selecting the matching brush textures again. Change the **Alignment** to **Box** and hit **Apply**. Then change the **Simple** scaling value to `4.0` and hit **Apply** again.

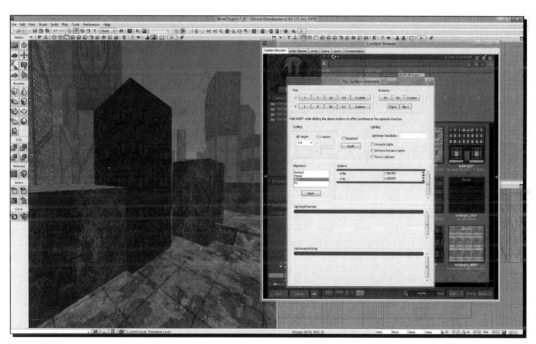

11. Apply textures to your level on buildings that you would like to see changed using the materials provided or with your own. Note that since the player will not see the roofs of our buildings we do not need to have a texture for them. This is seen in the following screenshot:

12. Save your project and start your game by clicking on the **Start Mobile Previewer** button.

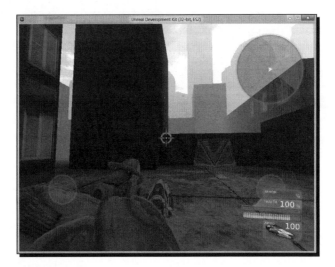

What just happened?

We now have a world that looks more polished with our own textures filling the world. With the same basic concepts here you can paint your brushes however you want!

Custom meshes

The static meshes that are included inside of UDK are fine, but if you want to create anything that is remotely different and detailed, chances are you will need to import custom meshes of your own.

For those creating their own models, there are various different tutorials on the internet for you to look at, but in general export your model as an FBX file and enable smoothing groups when exporting it and try to keep your models as low poly as possible. For more information on the creation of the models you can visit: `http://udn.epicgames.com/Three/DesigningForMobile.html`.

Time for action – importing custom objects

In our case, we would like to replace some of the BSP buildings that we created in the game with some simple static meshes that I created. We can do this as follows:

1. Open up the **Content Browser** by either selecting its icon or going to the **View** menu and selecting **View | Browser Windows | Content Browser**. Click on the **Import** button in the menu at the bottom of the window. Find the two building `.fbx` files, select them and then click on **Open**. In the window that pops up set the package with the same name that you created before and click on **OK**, saying yes if it asks you to import the entire package. This is seen in the following screenshot:

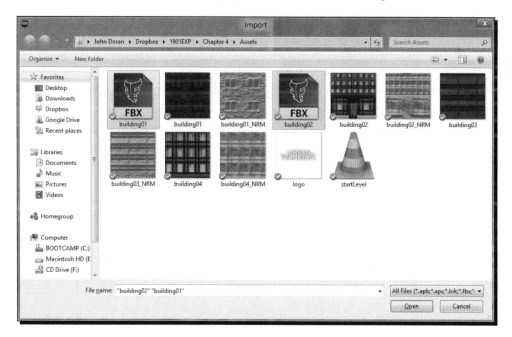

2. Right-click on the package name on the left-hand side of the **Content Browser** and save our package by selecting **Save** in the menu. Double-click on the first building in order to enter its properties, as shown in the following screenshot:

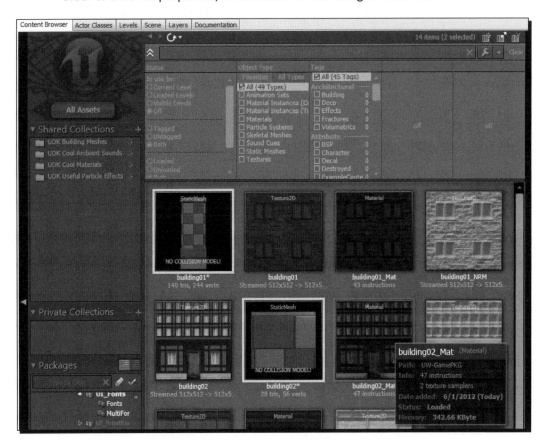

3. With the **Static Mesh Editor** open go back into the **Content Browser** and left-click on building01_Mat file. Inside the Properties under **LODInfo.[0].Elements.[0]** in **Material** click on the green arrow pointing towards the left to set the Material to the one we selected, as shown in the following screenshot:

4. On the menu at the top of the **Static Mesh Editor** click **Collision | 6DOP Simplified Collision** in order to make the building collide with objects.

If you would like to see the collision generated for the object you can click on the icon in the panel at the top of the screen that looks like it has a red box around it. You can also import your own custom collision that you created in your favorite modeling program. For more information about that, visit: `http://udn.epicgames.com/Three/FBXStaticMeshPipeline.html#Collision`

5. Double-click on **building02** to enter the **Static Mesh Editor** and repeat steps 3 and 4 using `building02_Mat` as the material to use.

6. Back in our level find a building that is a similar shape to **building01**. Delete that brush and in its place right-click and select **Add Static Mesh : UWGamePKG. Building01**. Scale the object up till it fits the area of the object you deleted and move it down until it fits the ground or hit the *End* key, then click on **Rebuild All**.

7. Do the same for other buildings, and continue replacing brushes with the buildings at random intervals trying to make it so you can't see duplicates of them within the same frame or area.

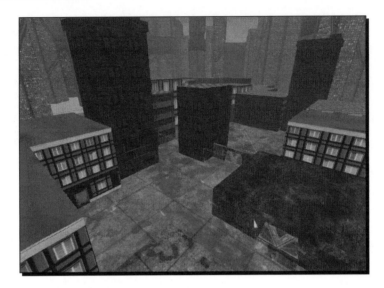

8. Turn on the **Emulate Mobile Feature** at this point to give you a better feel of what the game may look on the device. You can toggle the mode on and off by clicking on the little icon that looks like a phone to the left-hand side of the **Install on iOS Device** button.

9. Save your project and start your game by clicking on the **Start Mobile Previewer** button.

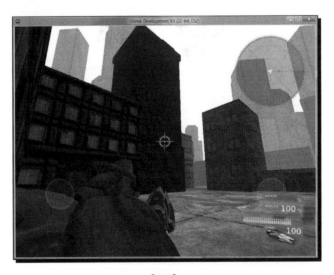

What just happened?

You now have all sorts of custom features added into your game giving you some great examples and now if you'd like to go in and bring in your own models you are free to do that as well!

Optimizations

There are a ton of resources on how to optimize your game and plenty of discussions on forums of the best ways to do things. In the following sections I will talk about different aspects that I use in order to optimize my games.

Console commands – statistics

One of the neat new additions to UDK in terms of mobiles is the fact that by holding four fingers on the screen at a time you can open up the console window. You can find a list of console commands you can use in UDK at `http://udn.epicgames.com/Three/ConsoleCommands.html`. Also note that the values you may see on the PC are in no way an indicator of how things will be on an iOS device so be sure to do your testing by either using the four-finger process or calling the `Console Command` in Kismet. The following are some of the stats that I found most useful when debugging projects.

stat fps

The easiest one to see why we would want it, the FPS counter tells us how many frames per second our game runs. 24 frames per second is the accepted threshold where animation becomes possible, if it is much less, the visuals seems jagged or our brains can tell that they are just images. 30 FPS is an accepted standard in most Unreal games, though some have been able to do 60.

stat game

This shows statistics related to the time it takes to run different parts of the game, which may make it easier to see which sections of the game are taking the longest to run with the number of checkmarks, and the time it takes to do certain things such as Kismet and UnrealScript.

stat memory

This shows how much memory is being used by each individual section of the game. The larger the memory, the more processing power it takes to use and the larger your game will be. Apple only allows you to download apps that are 50 MB or less through 3G/4G, so having an app with a size larger than this will force it to be downloaded through WiFi, which will probably be how your game will wind up, due to the size of UDK, but it still is a good idea to keep your memory footprint low.

stat es2

OpenGL ES2 is the iOS rendering device and while inside the Mobile Previewer it may crash when run on an iOS device. You can see useful data in terms of how many draw calls are done as well other useful stats to see. Try to keep your draw calls down as low as you can as it will probably be the thing that slows your game down the most.

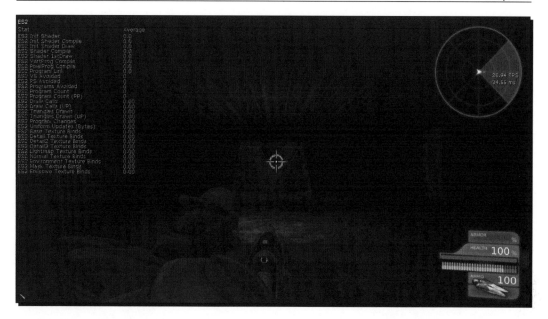

Combining meshes

Speaking of draw calls, we have just learned how to create meshes in our game project earlier in this chapter. When wanting to optimize our game, it may be a good idea to combine similar meshes that contain the same texture together as long as it is still low poly. Having fewer meshes reduces the amount of draw calls that need to be made. In the same regard, reduce the amount of materials that you use on an individual object, constraining yourself to only one Material per object if you possibly can. Using multiple materials on an object at the very least doubles the amount of memory needed to compute and run it, which is not a very good thing when you're trying to make your game as efficient as possible.

Precomputed visibility

Hardware occlusion queries are appealing in games because they work in completely dynamic scenes, but sadly iOS devices do not support occluding objects. By occluding objects I mean that if the player does not see an object, the game can skip drawing that object. While our little game happens to run fine, larger projects will want to make use of this feature as it can greatly improve runtimes. To learn how to set precomputed visibility in your game, see: http://udn.epicgames.com/Three/PrecomputedVisibility.html.

Streaming volumes

While we're on the topic of larger levels, by far the best way in my opinion to create larger levels is by using streaming volumes. What that basically does is make it so that when you enter a certain area of the world, a level will be loaded. However, in the transition between levels there may be a time when more than one level is open which will lower your frame rate drastically. I personally create small areas in between my larger levels that contain parts of both levels that make the transition more seamless and less of a hog on memory all at once. For more information on streaming volumes and how to set it up, check out:

`http://udn.epicgames.com/Three/LevelStreamingVolumes.html`

Debugging

Being able to debug your game doesn't seem that important, until something in your game breaks. Having a firm grounding in ways to see what is going on in your game will definitely help you later on down the road as you delve into projects of your own.

Comment your code

This is something that was drilled into me in college and advice I am very thankful for taking. Chances are that while working on any large project you are not going to be touching a particular sequence in Kismet every day. Weeks are going to go by and you are going to forget why certain things were done. This is just as applicable to Kismet as it is to any other kind of programming language, and thankfully Unreal gives us the ability to make it simple to tell others what is going on. Selecting multiple objects and then right-clicking and selecting **Comment** allows you to type something in, which can give a clue into what a group of Kismet nodes are used for, such as this reworked Player Spawned event:

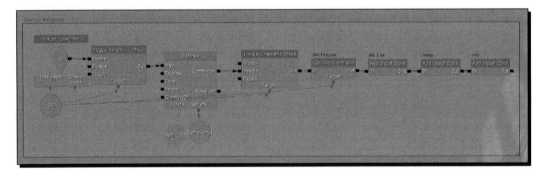

I also added in object comments at the end of the different input zones, for example I did this when I put in the push button example, except I didn't trigger the output on the screen. Now it is used so that when I glance at the code I know what I'm adding. Cleaning up the code that we did during the project I came up with this:

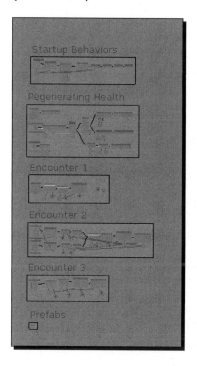

Even with a glance it is always better to look at than having no guidance at all, making it simple to find what you're looking for either there or in any of the subsequences we created. You could even take this idea further, creating subsequences for each of the different items, but that's more of finding what you're comfortable with and getting accustomed to your own style of doing things.

Captain's log

Now, there will come a time where you are sure everything is correct and all of your Kismet actions are being called. Well, there's one way to be sure of the value that something is, and that's by logging it and displaying what the data is at runtime. You can create a **Log** action by going into **New Action | Misc | Log**. From there you can right-click on the object and select **Expose Variable** and choose a type of something you'd like to get the value of. With that if you set the **Target** to **Player 0** and the other item to some of that type, when you play the game and it is called, the game will display what it is. For example when I add a **Log** action to this event:

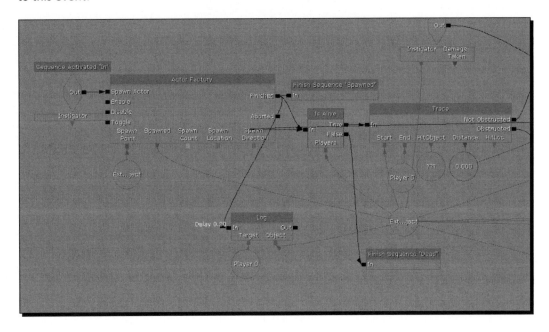

`UTPawn_0` gets displayed in the log. This is the name of the object that we put in the object variable link of the Log action.

Being able to make sure that an object has a value you think it should have is one of the most obvious ways to tell if something is wrong, other than it not being called at all, of course.

Summary

Our game is now effectively our own, or at least on its way to being our own. With this knowledge I'm confident that you are more than ready to build your game to be as large as you'd like as well as inputting all sorts of custom stuff into the game. We've specifically learned how to:

- Create a main menu for our game with input
- Add audio on mobile UDK for our game
- Import custom textures to our game
- Create a materials for both PC and iOS to use
- Add static meshes on Mobile UDK for our game
- Optimize and Debug our game on the iOS

Now that we've learned how to import all of your custom content to your heart's desire, we need to complete our main game in the next chapter. We will go over how to take the game that we created and get it onto the iTunes store and the steps that it requires as well to make your game a success!

8
Publishing and Monetizing Your Game

We now have our game in a finished state with a fully featured level and we have playtested it and refined it on the computer, but at some point you're going to want to get the game on your iOS device. This chapter will be all about that: getting the game first on our own iOS device, and then going all the way to publishing on the App Store.

In this chapter we shall:

- ◆ Learn about the process of getting your game onto an iOS device
- ◆ Go through the process of deploying the game on your own iOS device
- ◆ Customize our game's icons when viewed from our device as well as the App Store
- ◆ Discuss the playtesting process and learn how to do playtesting sessions of your own
- ◆ Discuss the current royalties model Epic Games has in place for UDK-developed iOS titles
- ◆ Learn how to link Game Center into our games for a fuller social experience
- ◆ Explore using in-game ads for monetization
- ◆ Go through the process of uploading your game on the iTunes store

It's a lot of stuff to go through, so at the very least I will give you an overview of the most used options available and what UDK has in place to make things happen. So with that, let's get started!

Before the magic happens

Very soon we will have your game running on your device and it will be fantastic, but before we get to that point, there are a few things we have to make sure of at first. First of all, you will need to own an iOS device (which we will assume you have) in order to test it out first. You will need to set up provisioning for your game, which we will discuss later, and finally, you will also need to have a developer account, which we will talk about first.

Registering as an iOS developer

In order to put a game in the App Store using UDK you must first be a registered iOS developer. The process is relatively painless, however at the time of this writing Apple charges $99 a year for the privilege of being a developer. If at any time you let your subscription end, all of the apps you've created will be removed as well. If you are not a developer yet, you will need to register at `https://developer.apple.com/programs/ios/`.

On that page you will see a button that says **Enroll Now**. From there, Apple has done a good job to make it as simple as possible by filling information out and following the menus. Upon completion, you will have a developer account.

Setting up provisioning

In order to even test games on an iOS device you are required to have the correct generation of keys, certificates, and mobile profiles which is what is called **provisioning**. Apple requires that any device that runs any app must be set up with a provisioning profile. The **Unreal iOS Configuration Wizard** makes the process of setting up the provisioning process easier, though it still requires the use of the iOS provisioning portal on Apple's developer website for certain aspects.

Time for action – creating new provisioning

In order to get our game on our own iOS device, we need to create a provisioning profile. With that in mind, let's get it started!

1. Connect your iOS device to your computer via USB. Make sure you have enough free space on your device to install the game.

2. To the left-hand side of the **Mobile Previewer** button, you should see an icon that looks like a mobile device with a red arrow pointing upwards. If this is the first time you are doing this, the **Unreal iOS Configuration Wizard** should come up.

If, for any reason, it doesn't appear, you can also find it in the `\Binaries\IPhone` folder inside your UDK Installation with the name `IPhonePackager.exe`. You can also run it from the **Unreal Frontend**, but that will be discussed later in the chapter. This is shown in the following screenshot:

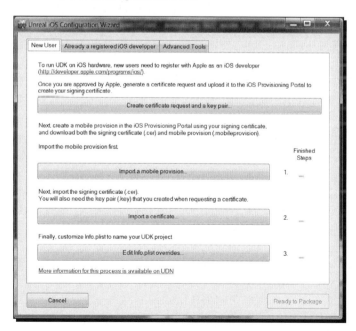

3. From the menu click on the **Create certificate request and a key pair...** button to bring up a new menu. Fill in the fields with the information requested, making sure to use the e-mail you registered as an iOS developer in the **Email Address** field and the **Common Name** being your first and last name or your company name. As you finish something, you will notice green checkmarks showing up as shown in the following screenshot:

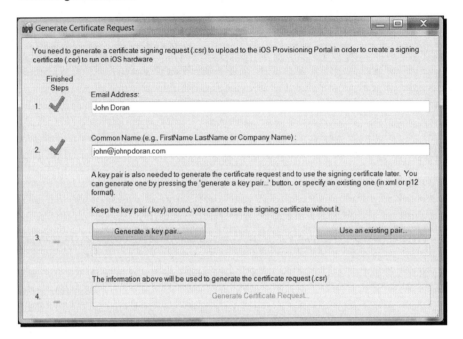

4. Click on the **Generate a key pair...** button to create a key pair file. This will open up a file-saving dialog, which will allow you to save the file in a known folder. As this will be the same for all of your projects it would be a good idea to place it in your UDK installation folder in something like `C:\UDK\Developer Files`.

5. Afterwards click on the **Generate Certificate Request** button which will also create a file for you to save. Save it in the same directory you created earlier.

While this method will work now in allowing us to run the game on our own iOS device, we will be required to import the certificate file into our keychain on a Mac computer when you want to publish your app on the App Store.

 The following steps assume you have Firefox or Safari as your web browser. While it may work fine using others, if you have a problem I would use either of these two options.

6. Open up your web browser and visit the Apple developer's site at `https://developer.apple.com/` and click on the **iOS Dev Center** option. The following screenshot shows this:

7. Click on the **Log in** button and enter in your credentials. When the **iOS Dev Center** comes up, click on the **iOS Provisioning Portal** link on the toolbar at right-hand side as shown in the following screenshot:

8. On **the iOS Provisioning Portal** page, there will be a picture of an iPhone beside some text with a button underneath it saying **Launch Assistant**. Click on that button. The following screen will appear:

9. A new setup should start. Click on the **Continue** button to start.

10. At this point you need to create an **App ID**, which is an identifier that will allow iOS to communicate with your app, such as for push notifications. You will need to also choose a display name for the app, which is the readable name which will be used in various places. Once you type an **App ID**, click on **Continue**.

11. Next, you need to specify what device you will be playing the game on. Enter a description for the device, such as `iPad`. Underneath you will see a place to enter your **Device ID**. While it is possible to obtain the **Device ID** using Xcode on a Mac, it may be simpler at this time to just open up **iTunes** and find the ID there.

12. Open up **iTunes**. Click on your device to bring up its menu. From there click on the **Serial Number** option to change the value to show its identifier (UDID). After it is shown click on **Edit | Copy Identifier** (UDID). Refer to the following screenshot:

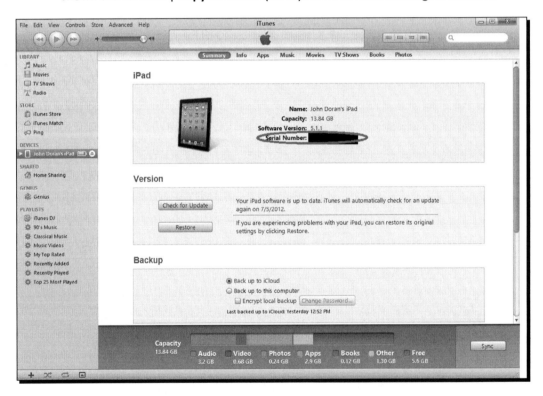

13. Paste the code into your **Device ID** property in the previous menu and hit **Continue**.

14. You should now be brought to the **Generate Certificate Signing Request** step. Hit continue to skip this page as we already created a **Certificate Request** inside of the **Configuration Wizard** earlier in step 5.

15. At the **Submit Certificate Signing Request** step click on the **Browse** button and locate the certificate (the `.csr` file) inside the folder, where you placed it during step 5 and hit **Continue**.

16. At this point you will be asked for a **Profile Description**. This is a name that will be used to identify a particular provision, such as if you had an iPhone and an iPad and wanted to try the game on both. With that finished, click on the **Generate** button. This is shown in the following screenshot:

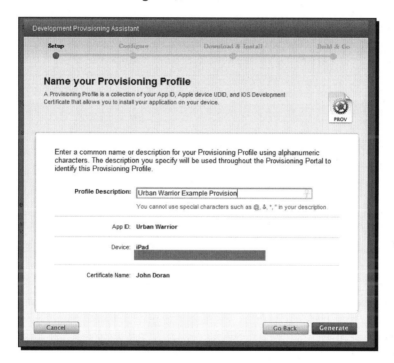

17. When the next page fully loads, your provisioning profile will be completed. Once the large green checkmark appears on the bottom step, click on **Continue**.

18. Click on the **Download** button on the next screen and save the file into the same place you put the other two files we created this chapter.

19. Once you have completed the download, click on the **Continue** button. Click on **Continue** again to pass the **Download & Install Your Provisioning Profile** as we won't need it now, but we will when we want to submit our game to the App Store.

20. At this step you should see **Download & Install Your Development Certificate**. We need this as well, so save the file into our important files' folder.

21. Once the file is completed, click on **Continue**. Click on **Continue** again to pass the **Download & Install Your Development Certificate** as we won't need it now, but we will when we want to submit our game to the **App Store**.

22. Continue past the **Install your iOS application with Xcode** page as we will not be using it when creating a game with UDK.

23. At this point you should have completed the **Provisioning Assistant**, and we can click on **Done** on the next page to exit the assistant. This is shown in the following screenshot:

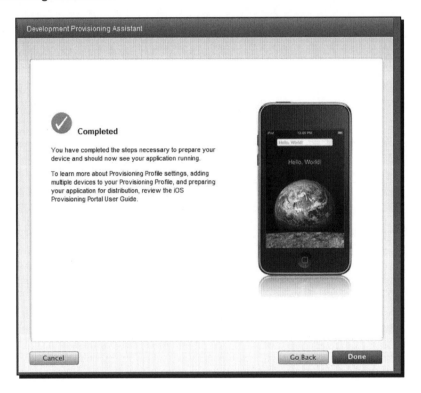

24. Back in the **Unreal iOS Configuration Wizard** go to the **New User** tab. Click on the **Import a mobile provision...** button to import the provisioning file that you saved in our important documents' folder. It should be the only file of its type the folder. This is shown in the following screenshot:

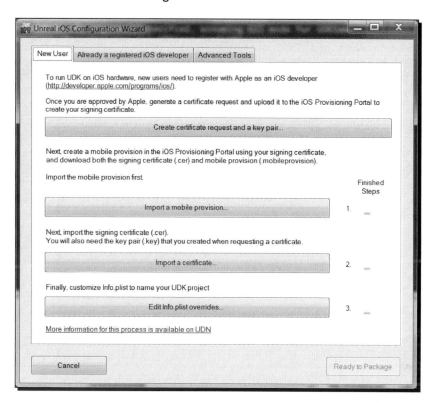

25. Next, click on **Import a certificate...** to import the developer certificate. Once selected, it will ask you to import the key pair file that you made when generating the certificate request. Click on **OK** and select the key pair file. At this point, we should have two green checkmarks on the right-hand side.

26. Click the **Edit Info.plist overrides...** button to open the **Customize Info.plist** window. Under **Bundle Display Name,** type the name you want your game to be on the iOS device. You will want to use a small name to make sure that it will fit within the space the OS will provide, something like Urban Warrior would work. In **Bundle Name** type a condensed version of the name. This is what iOS will use to identify the app, I used Urban Warrior. In **Bundle Identifier** type the same thing that was used in the provisioning file, as stated in the packager dialog. Click on **Save Changes**. This is shown in to the following screenshot:

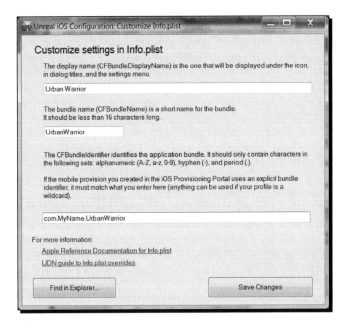

27. With all of the checkmarks completed, click on the **Ready to Package** button. If you got to this page by clicking on the icon I mentioned earlier, the game should be pushed to your device after a period of time. Otherwise, click on the **Install on iOS device** button. After a period of time you should see a popup telling you that the game has been deployed. This can be seen in the following screenshot:

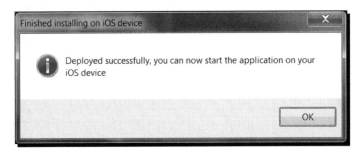

28. After the game is pushed to your device open up your iPad and touch the icon of your game **Urban Warrior** as shown in the previous screenshot. You will see the following screenshot:

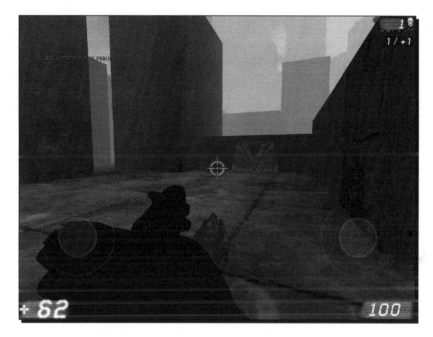

What just happened?

Our game is now on our very own iOS device. It took a lot of steps to get there, but we finally made it! Every time I get to play something that I created on a new console, I always get a warm feeling inside of accomplishment, and I hope you're feeling the same. Congratulations on getting this far, you are now officially an iOS Developer!

Custom Graphics

While Epic provides graphics to be used with their games being used on iOS, one of the easy things we can do to make our game more our own is by customizing the graphics shown on the iOS version of our game. iOS apps use a collection of different icon images of many different sizes to support the large variety of items that we support. Replacing these images with your own custom images will make it so that when you package the game, using either the **Unreal Frontend** or the **Install on iOS Device** command, it will use those assets. The folder that contains those assets would be at `UDKGame/Build/IPhone/Resources/Graphics/`. As of the time of writing, if you are creating a **Universal App** these are the possible graphics you can/should use:

Image Size (px)	File Name	Used For
512x512	`iTunesArtwork`	Ad Hoc iTunes
57x57	`Icon.png`	App Store and the Home screen on iPhone/iPod touch
114x114	`Icon@2x.png`	Home screen for iPhone 4 High Resolution
72x72	`Icon-72.png`	App Store and Home screen on iPad
50x50	`Icon-Small-50.png`	Spotlight on iPad
29x29	`Icon-Small.png`	Settings on iPad and iPhone, and spotlight on iPhone
58x58	`Icon-Small@2x.png`	Spotlight and settings for iPhone 4 High Resolution

 To get the latest up-to-date knowledge on the sizes for icons that you are required to have or would need to use for different devices visit `https://developer.apple.com/library/ios/#qa/qa2010/qa1686.html`.

When creating icons, I find it easier to start from something large and then work down in size, in order to not have any pixelation in my artwork. I took the liberty of making some sample icons that you are free to use in your own projects. Here's an example of what it looks like:

Playtesting on the device

At this point, we have played our game using the Mobile Previewer with and without the aid of the UDK Remote, but it is an entirely different thing to actually play the game on your own device. For one thing your hands are now on the screen so **HUD** elements that you created may be hard to see, such as the buttons we created. It is also a very good idea to have other people playtest your game and give you feedback.

Why playtest?

Playtesting is one of the most important things in deciding the success of a video game. However it is an area that is often way overlooked during the game creation process so I want to stress how important it is to do. Playtesters are the voice of how a normal person is going to react to your game. It is important that you take what they say seriously. They are also the people that are going to find and exploit anything they can get their hands on within your world, and you will find things that you never thought were possible in your game.

When building your project, it is incredibly important to prototype as early as you can and get a feel if what you are working on is actually fun to your target audience. There is no secret formula to create fun (and thankfully so because game designers would be out of a job) but you can apply principles that you have learned from other products, as well as your own creativity to see if it works. That being said, you should playtest your game more than any other person before you set the game in front of your gaming group. After all, if your gaming group doesn't like what you're doing, chances are your App Store reviews aren't going to be as amazing as you think they'd be.

How to playtest

Large companies devote a large amount of resources into their playtesting, creating labs with cameras that record a playtester from many different angles, as well as recording input and player behavior, trying to turn it into a science. But, unlike those companies, I know for a fact that I can't afford to do that, so instead I go with the next best thing. There are a lot of different ways to conduct a playtesting session.

When I do playtesting sessions myself, I typically have a questionnaire that I have players fill out after they have played the game. A lot of the questions are circling a number from 1-10 talking about if the game was too difficult, the goals were hard to understand, and other assorted things that you want to figure out. I also leave a large blank at the end of additional thoughts, as those who are heavily invested will no doubt have tons of things to say to you.

For those who are still in school, I find a very easy way to get people to play your game is ordering a couple pizzas and giving someone a slice for playing your game. You could create your own website and have visitors fill out a questionnaire after playing your game. There are also many online communities of people who are always eager to try new games out and give feedback such as ModDB/IndieDB, at `http://www.moddb.com/` and `http://www.indiedb.com/` though it may be an issue for getting iOS specific feedback. At the very least talking to friends and handing them your iPad is another way to get someone to play your game, though your friends and family may be biased in their reviews.

It is also very important that you have people play your game without your input. Most designers believe that they have covered every possible thing in their rulebook, but it is almost guaranteed that something has been forgotten. In level design it is important to see what directions that players go in and if they are being guided in the correct way. At no point in a game should players feel stupid. Having games that are not complete is a sure way of making a player feel that they just wasted their money on an incomplete product. There have been times that I have played a game that had no way to actually win if you followed the rules included.

Try to have a thick skin, and thank everyone for their feedback; not everyone is going to like your game, but if you see a trend forming chances are you may want to adjust the game. Playtesters are going to suggest changes and it will be your decision whether or not those changes are really worth having or not. There are times when it is for a player's own good or for balance's sake that things are the way they are. Another important thing to remember is to playtest often, as you need to see if the changes you made are helping or not and rinse and repeat until you're satisfied to publish.

Commercialization

With your project mostly finished it may be a good time to look at the possibilities of commercialization of your game. As this book is a beginner's book, I will not delve too much into specifics for implementing all of the features possible for these services; it would be large enough for its own book, but I will be going over what can be done and give some resources for any budding developer that just has to have *x* feature in their game.

 Note that most of these features will require UnrealScript input of some sort into your game in order to implement it, and as this book does not cover UnrealScript you will have to do a lot of research on your own, but the links I've given are what I used to learn it so I feel quite certain that you can do the same as well.

Licensing UDK

UDK is free to use for non-commercial or educational purposes. If you are going to use the UDK for any commercial purpose, or have ads of any kind in your game you have to apply for a license with Epic Games at `http://www.udk.com/licensing`. The terms of the license as of writing is $99 up-front with a 0% royalty for the company's first $50,000 in revenue and 25% for all remaining gained revenue. As we are publishing our game on iOS, Apple takes a cut of the cost receiving 30% leaving you with 70% of the profits. If your app gained $100 of sales but you only received 70%, the royalty is calculated on the $70 that you did receive. And while it may seem like 25% may be a lot, if you sold your app at $1 it would take you selling 71,428 apps to get that mark.

In-game advertisements

Those who want to make their game free to download while still wanting to make a profit, could add in-game advertisements to their game. Apple has an entire network called **iAd** which can be added to your game with only a few lines of code. It is important to note that you will have to purchase a license for UDK in order to distribute your game with Ads and the revenue that you generate with those ads is revenue. For more information about adding ads to your game visit `http://udn.epicgames.com/Three/InGameAds.html`.

In-app purchases

One of the other ways to make money on your game is by having certain things unlocked, by making purchases after a game is purchased. An example of this could be access to certain levels and/or features. One thing to be careful about is the fact that people may complain about not getting a full version of the game in this way. A possible solution for this is to have in-app purchases for purely cosmetic things, such as a different character or outfit.

 For more information about implementing a micro-transaction system into your game visit `http://udn.epicgames.com/Three/MicroTransactions.html`.

Bringing everyone together with Game Center

Game Center is Apple's online gaming network. Gamers with iOS devices can use this service in order to compete against each other for achievements, play multiplayer, and even voice chat with each other.

To add Game Center to your game, simply go to the `IPhoneEngine.ini` file located in your UDK folder at `\UDKGame\Config\IPhone\` and set the value of `bDisableGameCenter` to false as follows:

```
[OnlineSubsystemGameCenter.OnlineSubsystemGameCenter]
bDisableGameCenter=false
```

However, if you plan on using leader boards or achievements, it is a little more complicated as you will need to dive into UnrealScript, to implement the ability to get an achievement in the game.

 For more information visit `http://udn.epicgames.com/Three/GameCenter.html`.

iCloud integration

Apple's **iCloud** is a form of storage that saves data that can be accessed from any iOS device that a person owns. This could be a prime way of creating save files for your game, saving the player's progress.

 For more information visit `http://udn.epicgames.com/Three/CloudDocumentStorage.html`.

Facebook/Twitter integration

Another feature that the iOS version of UDK has is the ability to tweet or post on your Facebook page. It can make full use of Facebook's API being able to retrieve your friends list and many other things. To find out more about either of these two things, visit `http://udn.epicgames.com/Three/TwitterIntegration.html` or `http://udn.epicgames.com/Three/FacebookIntegration.html` respectively.

Bringing our game to the world

Now that our game is in peak shape, and is the next big iOS hit, let's publish it for the world to see; or at least Apple's approval staff. At this point, you will be required to have a Mac computer in order to complete the process.

Time for action – requesting a Distribution Certificate

The first action to take is to create a distribution provisioning. This is different from the one we created earlier because it will be used for placement on multiple devices.

1. Go to the **iOS Provisioning Portal** page on the Apple developer's site and instead of using the launcher click on **Certificates** on the left-hand side toolbar as shown in the following screenshot:

2. Click on the **Distribution** tab and request a new distribution certificate by clicking the **Request Certificate** button on the right-hand side of that page.

3. Scroll to the bottom of the page and find the `.csr` file that we created earlier and click the **Submit** button. We will then return to the **Distribution** tab from before and after a period you will see the certificate say **Issued**. This is shown in the following screenshot:

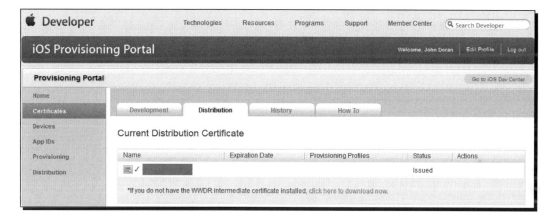

4. Switch tabs to **Development** and back to **Distribution**. Upon coming back you will notice that the **Actions** tab has a download button. Click on it and save the file to the same place as the rest of our files.

5. Next we need to create a **Distribution Profile**. Click on the **Provisioning** section of the **iOS Provisioning Portal** and the **Distribution** tab in much the same way we did before. Click on the **New Profile** button to bring us to the **Create iOS Distribution Provisioning Profile** page.

6. Leave the **Distribution** method at **App Store**. The **Ad Hoc** option is there if you are trying to distribute the app on your own, such as if you were creating an internal application for your business.

7. Under **Profile Name** type a name to identify the profile to you in the **iOS Provisioning Profile**, like `Urban Warrior Provision`.

8. **Distribution Certificate** should list the certificate that we created previously. Under **App ID** select our app, and leave devices blank as it is only used in **Ad Hoc** distribution.

9. Click on the **Submit** button and it will take you back to the **Distribution** tab of the **Provisioning** home page. This is shown in the following screenshot:

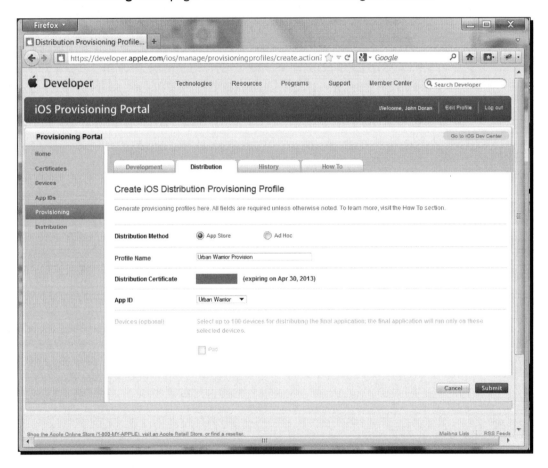

10. On the page you will see the **Provision** with a status of **Pending**. Switch to the **Development** tab and back to **Distribution** and you will notice it will now be displayed as **Active**. Download the file to our folder of items. This is shown in the following screenshot:

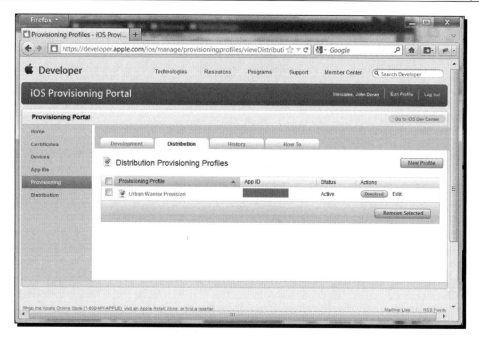

11. Open the **iPhonePackager** tool by going to your `Binaries\IPhone` folder inside your UDK installation by double-clicking on the file `IPhonePackager.exe`. This is shown in the following screenshot:

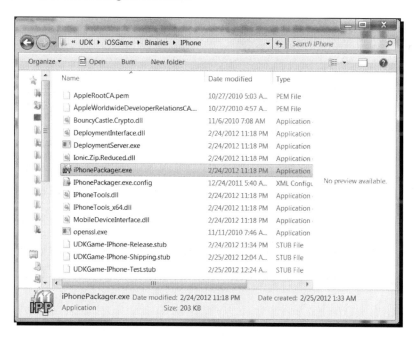

12. The program should start with the **Advanced Tools** tab highlighted. Click on **Provision and certificate tools...** to bring up the **Signing Tool**.

13. From there, click on **Import a mobile provision...** to import the distribution file using the file dialog.

14. Next click on **Import a certificate...** and use the file dialog to locate your distribution certificate (probably named ios_distribution.cer). After that a message box will ask you for your key file. Click on **OK** and then select your key pair file. Click on **Refresh List** to see the certificate to be displayed. This is shown in the following screenshot:

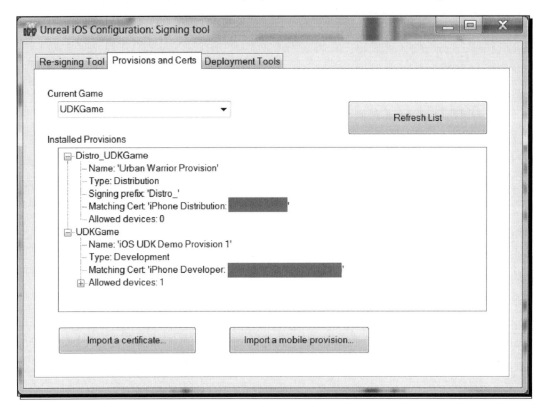

15. Make sure UDK is closed and open the **Unreal Frontend** by going to your **Binaries** folder in your UDK installation and double-clicking on the UnrealFrontend.exe application. Make sure that the editor program is closed as well because if it isn't, then you are almost guaranteed to have errors in the next few steps.

16. Click on the large button on the right-hand side side of your **Frontend** that says something similar to **UDKGame on PC(Shipping 32) | Cook/Make/Sync with ...** From the options in the menu, select the **IPhone** for the **Platform**, **Shipping_32** for the **Game Config**, **ReleaseScript** for the **Script Config**, and **Shipping_32** for the **Cook/Make Config**. Click on **OK** to save your settings.

When you are completely finished with your game, it would be a good idea to use the **FinalReleaseScript** option as it will run better due to removing assert checks and log information. Refer to the following screenshot:

17. In the **Mobile** section underneath the large button, change the **Packaging Mode** to **Distribution**.

18. Click the **Add...** button and type the name of all the levels that you want to have in your game clicking **Add Selected Maps** to add the map to your game. This is shown in the following screenshot:

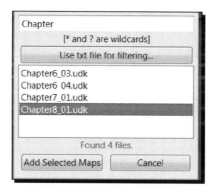

19. Make sure the **Override Default** option is checked and select your first level to be your first level to play. This is shown in the following screenshot:

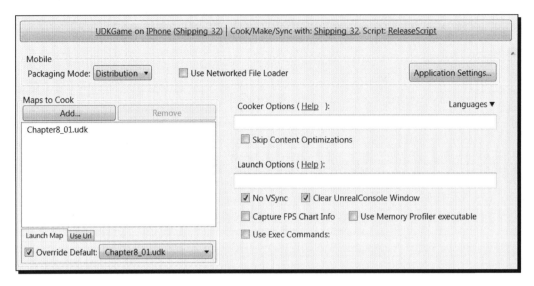

If you would not like to use the **Override Default** option, you can also set the default level in the DefaultEngine.ini file.

20. Click underneath the **Deploy** button and select **Step Enabled** to skip deploying to your device, as a distribution build can't be put on your normal device. If you would like to have a full build on your device, change the **Packaging Mode** to **Default**. This is shown in the following screenshot:

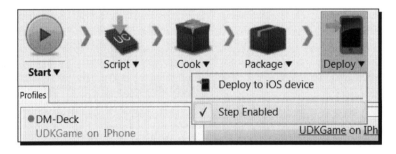

21. With all of the options set, click on the arrow beside the word start and select **Clean and Full Recook** and wait for the commands to all execute. This is shown in the following screenshot:

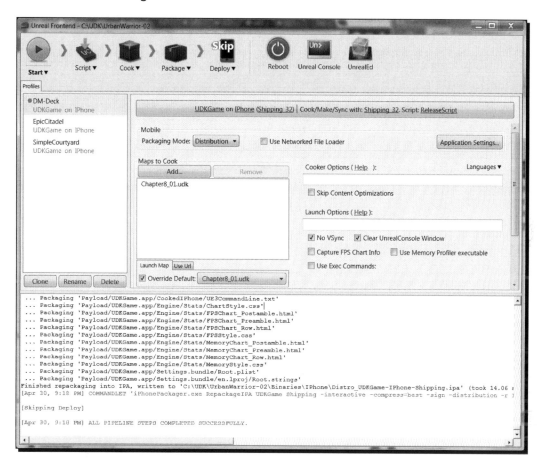

22. If everything went well, you should have a `.ipa` file named `Distro_UDKGame` inside you `\Binaries\IPhone\Shipping-iphoneos\UDKGame` which you will want to save to a jump drive or similar, because we will need it when we move to our Mac computer section of this.

23. Back on Firefox/Safari, we next need to go to the **iTunes Connect** section of the **iOS Dev Center** which is located directly beneath the **iOS Provisioning Portal** that we used before. This is shown in the following screenshot:

24. Log in with your credentials, if it asks you to and agree to the **Terms of Service**. On the main page click on the **Manage your Applications** selection which is the first button on the right-hand side of your screen. This is shown in the following screenshot:

25. Click on the **Add New App** button on the top on the left-hand side. If this is your first application, you will be brought to the **New Application** page, where you need to come up with a company name, so be careful, because once you create it you are stuck with it, so be sure it is what you want.

26. Next you will have a number of different things to fill out. Under **Default Language** set it as English. Under **App Name** type the name of the app you would like, such as Urban Warrior. Under **SKU Number** type any number, but remember that every game that you create has to have a different number associated with it. Under **Bundle ID** select the **Bundle ID** that we created previously and in the **Bundle ID Suffix** type value that will match your info.plist file, which you set previously in the IPhonePackager in the **Edit Info.plist overrides...** section on the **New User** tab. Once completed hit **Continue**. This is shown in the following screenshot:

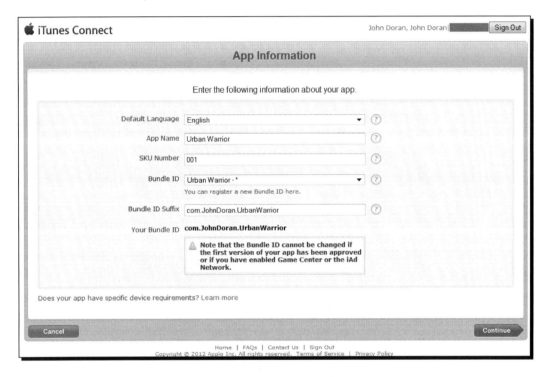

27. Now select a date and price tier for your application to use, as well as a discount for educational purchasers if you would like there to be one. You may also select specific App Stores you would like to sell your app to. Remember if you do not set your price tier to free, you will have to pay UDK a licensing fee. Once you are finished click on **Continue**.

28. In the next section, there are plenty of metadata options to fill out that are specific to the game that you are working so them with your best judgment.

29. You will be required to upload images and screenshots of your game for both the iPhone/iPod Touch and iPad as well as a large icon that is 512(x)512.

A tip is to take screenshots from your actual device, by holding the power and home keys at the same time for a brief period and releasing. You should see the screen flash and in the **Photos** app you should see a picture of what you were doing. You can e-mail this picture to yourself ahead of time, to upload at this section.

30. When you are finished click on the **Save** button to save the app's information. This will take you to the **App Summary** page for the app. This is shown in the following screenshot:

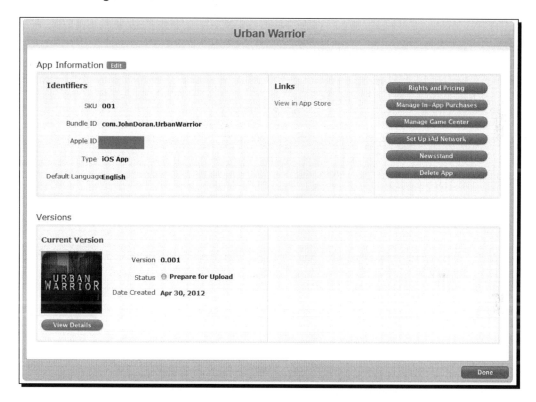

31. Click on the **View Details** button to go to the **App Details** page and from there click on **Ready to Upload Binary**. The menu will ask if you used cryptography at all to use your product in which you'll answer No and then hit **Save**. The menu will now show that you are ready to upload your binary using **Application Loader**; click on **Continue** and you'll be brought back to the main screen. Click on the **App Summary** text on the top left-hand side and then at the app summary page click on **Done** on the bottom right-hand side.

32. Go to your Mac computer and there is where we will complete the rest of the tutorial.

33. Install Xcode if you haven't already by using the App Store. You will see the next screenshot:

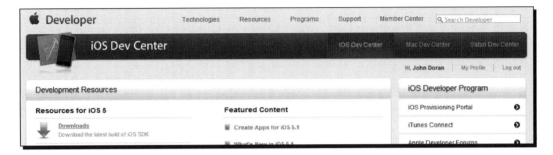

34. **Download and install the Application Loader** program by going to the **iTunes Connect** section of the site and clicking on **Download Application Loader** on the bottom tool bar. This is shown in the following screenshot:

35. After **Application Loader** is installed, open up **Spotlight** by pressing **Command** + *Space* and type the name of the program until it shows up and then click on it. This is shown in the following screenshot:

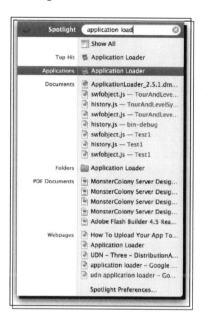

36. With the **Application Loader** opened enter your credentials and press **Next**. This is shown in the next screenshot:

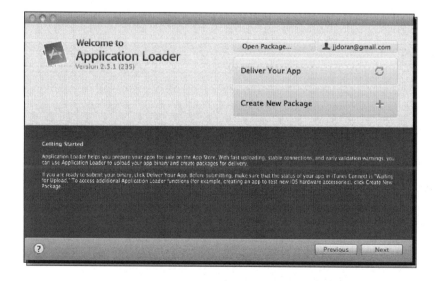

37. Click on the **Deliver Your App** button. From the menu that shows up, select your app and select the **Next** button. In the **Application Information** section click on the **Choose...** button and select your `.ipa` file and wait for it to complete.

38. When the upload completes click on **Next** and then **Done**. Feel free to log back in to **iTunes Connect** and go to the **Manage Your Applications** page to confirm that the app has been uploaded.

What just happened?

We have now submitted our app to Apple for review! You will get progress e-mails as the application passes through various phases of automated checking, finally reaching **Waiting for Review**, which means it is now in the process of getting reviewed by Apple. If anything happens you will get an e-mail, but the status will also be updated on the **iTunes Connect** website. Each time something is incorrect, you will have to hit **Ready to Upload** on the **iTunes Connect** website before the **Application Loader** can be used again.

Summary

With a firm handle on how to push our games to the App Store we've now covered everything that I set out to show you how to do within the confines of this book. We've specifically learned:

- About the process of getting your game onto an iOS device
- The process of deploying the game on your own iOS device
- How to customize our game's icons when viewed from our device as well as the App Store
- The playtesting process and learn how to do playtesting sessions of your own
- The current royalties model Epic Games has in place for UDK-developed iOS titles
- How to link Game Center into our games for a fuller social experience
- About the use of in-game ads for monetization
- The process of uploading your game on the iTunes store

It's hard to believe that in such a short time you've manage to complete so many different things! With the knowledge that you gained from this book you have all of the tools and knowledge to create some truly great projects. UDK is quite an amazing engine, and I know first-hand how much you can get out of it. So future app-creator, I wish you good luck and I'll see you in the App Store!

Pop Quiz Answers

Chapter 1: Getting Started on UDK with iOS

1	2	3	4
b	b	d	c

Chapter 2: Beginning Urban Warrior, a third-person Shooter

1	2	3
d	d	c

Chapter 4: Using Kismet and Matinee

1	2	3	4	5
c	a	b	d	d

Chapter 6: Brining It All Together

1	2	3
d	c	c

Index

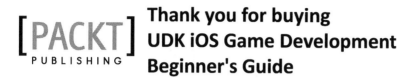

Thank you for buying
UDK iOS Game Development
Beginner's Guide

About Packt Publishing

Packt, pronounced 'packed', published its first book "Mastering phpMyAdmin for Effective MySQL Management" in April 2004 and subsequently continued to specialize in publishing highly focused books on specific technologies and solutions.

Our books and publications share the experiences of your fellow IT professionals in adapting and customizing today's systems, applications, and frameworks. Our solution-based books give you the knowledge and power to customize the software and technologies you're using to get the job done. Packt books are more specific and less general than the IT books you have seen in the past. Our unique business model allows us to bring you more focused information, giving you more of what you need to know, and less of what you don't.

Packt is a modern, yet unique publishing company, which focuses on producing quality, cutting-edge books for communities of developers, administrators, and newbies alike. For more information, please visit our website: www.PacktPub.com.

Writing for Packt

We welcome all inquiries from people who are interested in authoring. Book proposals should be sent to author@packtpub.com. If your book idea is still at an early stage and you would like to discuss it first before writing a formal book proposal, contact us; one of our commissioning editors will get in touch with you.

We're not just looking for published authors; if you have strong technical skills but no writing experience, our experienced editors can help you develop a writing career, or simply get some additional reward for your expertise.

Unreal Development Kit Game Programming with UnrealScript: Beginner's Guide

ISBN: 978-1-849691-92-5   Paperback:466 pages

Create games beyond your imagination with the Unreal Development Kit

1. Dive into game programming with UnrealScript by creating a working example game.

2. Learn how the Unreal Development Kit is organized and how to quickly set up your own projects.

3. Recognize and fix crashes and other errors that come up during a game's development.

4. A practical beginner's guide with fresh, fun writing that keeps you engaged as you learn game programming with UnrealScript

Unreal Development Kit Game Design Cookbook

ISBN: 978-1-849691-80-2   Paperback: 544 pages

Over 100 recipes to accelerate the process of learning game design with UDK book.

1. An intermediate, fast-paced UDK guide for game artists

2. The quickest way to face the challenges of game design with UDK

3. All the necessary steps to get your artwork up and running in game

Please check **www.PacktPub.com** for information on our titles

Unreal Development Kit 3

ISBN: 978-1-84969-052-2   Paperback:188 pages

A fun, quick, step-by-step guide to level design and creating your own game world.

1. Full of illustrations, diagrams, and tips for creating your first level and game environment.

2. Clear step-by-step instructions and fun practical examples.

3. Master the essentials of level design and environment creation

Unity 3.x Game Development by Example

ISBN: 978-1-849691-84-0   Paperback: 408 pages

A seat-of-your-pants manual for building fun, groovy little games quickly with Unity 3.x

1. Build fun games using the free Unity game engine even if you've never coded before

2. Learn how to "skin" projects to make totally different games from the same file – more games, less effort!

3. Deploy your games to the Internet so that your friends and family can play them

4. Packed with ideas, inspiration, and advice for your own game design and development

Please check **www.PacktPub.com** for information on our titles

Printed in Great Britain
by Amazon.co.uk, Ltd.,
Marston Gate.